CYPRIOT PLAINCHANT
OF THE
MANUSCRIPT TORINO, BIBLIOTECA NAZIONALE J. II. 9

MUSICOLOGICAL STUDIES AND DOCUMENTS

ARMEN CARAPETYAN, Ph. D.
General Editor

CYPRIOT PLAINCHANT
OF THE
MANUSCRIPT TORINO, BIBLIOTECA NAZIONALE J. II.9
RICHARD H. HOPPIN

MUSICOLOGICAL STUDIES AND DOCUMENTS

19

CYPRIOT PLAINCHANT

OF THE

MANUSCRIPT TORINO, BIBLIOTECA NAZIONALE J. II.9

A FACSIMILE EDITION
WITH
COMMENTARY
BY
RICHARD H. HOPPIN

1968
AMERICAN INSTITUTE OF MUSICOLOGY

CONTENTS OF COMMENTARY

CONTENTS OF FACSIMILE

PREFACE

This facsimile edition of the plainchant repertory in the Cypriot manuscript J. II. 9 in the Biblioteca Nazionale of Turin (Tu B) completes the modern republication of that remarkable witness to the musical life of the early fifteenth century [1]. For a number of reasons photographic reproduction has seemed not only the easiest but the best means of presenting this material. Transcription into modern note shapes, with or without stems, represents too great a departure from the external appearance of the original, and perhaps also from its internal substance, to be acceptable. Even the square notation of modern editions has been standardized and, so to speak, impersonalized to such an extent that its use would destroy the idiosyncratic and inconsistent notation of the Cypriot plainchant. Achieving an exact copy of that notation would present difficulties too horrendous to be contemplated.

It is hoped that the photographs will be nearly as legible as the manuscript itself. The musical notation presents no reading problems, and the texts, at least those that are set to music, are written in an exceptionally clear hand with a minimum of abbreviations. Damage to the manuscript, particularly in the first few folios, has made a few passages illegible, but for the most part there is little additional loss in the photographic process. But the interest of this section of the manuscript does not lie solely in the plainchant that it contains. In addition to numerous, and sometimes lengthy, texts without music, countless details including rubrics and abbreviated indications of traditional texts would be lost if only the chants themselves were presented. The two Offices are complete services, with all the necessary material or information for their liturgical performance. Total comprehension of these services should ideally be achieved through study of the

1 My transcriptions of the polyphonic music have been published in four volumes by the American Institute of Musicology under the title *The Cypriot-French Repertory of the Manuscript Torino, Biblioteca Nazionale J. II. 9.* (*Corpus Mensurabilis Musicae* 21 - CMM 21).

manuscript itself. In its absence, photographs provide the best and, indeed, the only substitute.

* * *

It is a pleasure to acknowledge here the considerable assistance without which this volume could not have been produced. In the first place I wish to thank Professor Stelio Bassi, Director of the Biblioteca Nazionale of Turin, for making it possible to obtain the negatives for the photographic reproductions. Thanks are also due to Professor Bassi and to the staff of the manuscript room in the Turin Library for the courteous and friendly reception that makes working there such a happy experience. A research grant from The Ohio State University provided both the free time and the means of revisiting Turin upon which depended the appearance of this volume. May it prove an adequate return for this confidence and this generosity.

Only an author knows the difficulty of acknowledging a wife's contribution. My debt to mine is incalculable and can never be repaid. All I can offer is my thanks and my deep appreciation of her willingness to go on living with an author in the house.

Columbus, Ohio

INTRODUCTION

A full description of the Manuscript Torino, Biblioteca Nazionale J. II. 9. (Tu B) would be inappropriate here, but we may recall some of the manuscript's physical characteristics in connection with this facsimile edition of the first twenty-eight folios [1]. Before it was damaged by fire in 1904, the folios of Tu B measured 39 x 28.3 cm., with the musical staves covering a space of 29.3 x 21.5 cm. In the sections devoted to polyphony this latter space contains twelve staves, whereas there are only eight staves to a page in folios 1-28. Throughout the manuscript the lines of the staves are drawn in red ink, and even in the plainchant section there are five lines for each staff, a peculiarity that may result from the generally wide range of the chant melodies.

Although the larger staves of the plainchant section give it the appearance of a choirbook, another peculiarity indicates that it was not primarily intended for use as such. In all the rest of the manuscript, the staves were obviously drawn in advance. Some are occasionally left empty at the bottom of a page, and they appear complete on folios that are otherwise blank. The staves in the plainchant section, on the other hand, were drawn only where needed to fit the individual chants. The reason for this procedure evidently lies in the frequent alternation of musical and nonmusical portions of the Offices, although it is maintained even in the continuous music of the Mass Ordinaries [2]. At least in the Offices, the appearance of staves only where needed is a first indication that we are dealing, not simply with another collection of chants for the *schola*, but rather with complete services that, for one reason or another, were deemed worthy of preservation.

The inclusion of a section of plainchant in a manuscript primarily

1 A more complete description is given in the Introduction to Vol. I of *The Cypriot-French Repertory of the Manuscript Torino, Biblioteca Nazionale J. II. 9.* (Rome, 1960). See also the article of H. Besseler cited in fn. 3.

2 See especially f. 23v and 28v.

devoted to polyphonic music is, in fact, so unusual that some attempt must be made to explain its presence. Fortunately, recorded facts concerning the Office of St. Hylarion make the probable explanation something more than mere conjecture. It has long been known that Janus, King of Cyprus, presented the Office to Pope John XXIII with a request for its approbation. The papal privilege sanctioning the Office was dated from Bologna on November 23, 1413 [3]. This specific connection with Cyprus, combined with the facts that the entire repertory is unique to Tu B and that further references to Cyprus appear in some of the motets and at least one secular song, has led to the assumption that the manuscript consists of music composed for, or at least assembled at, the Court of Cyprus. Since this assumption is demonstrably true for the Office of St. Hylarion, it is probably true also for the remaining material in the section devoted to plainchant: the Office of St. Anne, and the six cycles of the Mass Ordinary. The latter, as will be seen, are not the usual compilations of pre-existing chants. Instead, they appear to be newly composed for the purpose of making the Ordinary cycle a unified musical entity. The Office of St. Anne is less distinctive, although it may well have been composed to honor the name saint of Anne de Lusignan, daughter of King Janus and Charlotte de Bourbon. In any case, if the entire plainchant section of Tu B is assumed to contain Cypriot additions to the traditional plainchant repertory, its presence in a primarily polyphonic collection becomes much less mysterious. Only the hypothesis that the manuscript was designed as a monument to the total musical activity of Cyprus can explain both its careful organization and the disparate styles and types of music that it contains.

The present Commentary appended to this facsimile edition of Tu B, folios 1 to 28, is not intended to be a definitive study of either the music or the texts. It consists, rather, of a preliminary and somewhat tentative survey of two broad areas of inquiry suggested by these Offices and Mass cycles. The first of these areas concerns the relationship between the Cypriot services and the traditional liturgy and music of the western Church. Problems of liturgical forms, poetic structures, and appropriate musical styles are all involved here. Perhaps the chief result of even a cursory in-

[3] See *MD* XI (1957), 93. The sanction is also quoted in part by H. Besseler, "Studien zur Musik des Mittelalters", *Archiv für Musikwissenschaft* VII (1925), 209, n. 7.

vestigation of these problems is the revelation of the astonishing extent to which the Cypriot poets and composers follow the procedures of western Europe. In fact, apart from textual references to Cyprus, almost nothing can be found that betrays an insular origin. The plainchant section of Tu B thus corroborates the evidence of all the rest of the manuscript that Cypriot musicians were living in no peripheral backwater. On the contrary, they were as fully aware of the techniques being practised in the great musical centers of the West as they were capable of using those techniques with skill and taste.

The second area of inquiry is concerned with the analysis of the music itself and its relationship to both contemporary theory and practice. No attempt has been made to provide a systematic and complete treatment of this area. Indeed, such a treatment remains an impossibility until much more monophonic music of the fourteenth and fifteenth centuries is made available in modern publications. Scholars of plainchant tend to ignore almost completely the contributions of these centuries. Even the two preceding centuries are generally regarded as beginning the period of "decline" after the "Silver Age, the renaissance of plainsong activity that ended in the 12th century" [4]. Yet through the whole of the 15th century and even beyond a vast amount of new plainchant was still being composed. For the older, established services, of course, only the texts of the Mass Ordinary lent themselves to the frequent composition of new musical settings. The proliferation of new feast days and the constant addition of new saints to the local, national, or universal calendars continued unabated until the Council of Trent. All of these additions called for new chants for the Offices and perhaps also for the Proper of the Mass, as is the case in the Mass for St. Hylarion. Certainly for the sequences new melodies had to be composed or old ones adapted, and the more than 850 rhymed *historiae* published in the *Analecta Hymnica* (A H) all had to be provided with music [5]. However much of this music may have been lost, there still remains an enormous amount that has been almost totally neglected by modern scholars. Perhaps the emphasis on the reverse evolution of plainchant has been overdone. Until much more of this later chant is made available, at any rate, none can say that the production of praiseworthy

4 G. Reese, *Music in the Middle Ages* (New York, 1940), p. 125.

5 Vols. 5, 13, 17, 18, 24, 25, 26, 28, and 45a.

melodies ceased in the 12th century. And quite apart from any artistic treasures that may yet lie undiscovered, all of this later plainchant possesses tremendous historical interest. Specialists in the later Middle Ages and Renaissance have concerned themselves almost exclusively with polyphony, thus leaving an important aspect of composers' activities in these periods virtually unexplored. Yet even the small amount of music presented here makes it abundantly evident that later plainchant can teach us much about contemporary procedures of melodic composition. Questions of tonal organization, structural principles, and the varied use of standard motives and melodic formulas are all waiting to be investigated. It is impossible to believe that a detailed study of these questions, based on a much larger body of music, would not throw new light into many dark corners of our knowledge, even including our understanding of the creative processes involved in the composition of polyphony. It might also provide the most satisfactory starting point to begin developing those tools for the stylistic analysis of melody of which musicology has been so long in need.

No such high purposes are intended here. The most that can be hoped is that these few examples of plainchant from the early 15th century will not be the last of their type to be made available. Perhaps it may also be hoped that the unanswered questions posed in this Commentary will provide a stimulus for the thoroughgoing study that later plainchant so richly deserves.

STRUCTURE OF THE OFFICES

The structure underlying the Offices of both St. Hylarion and St. Anne follows the common usage for non-monastic Offices in the Middle Ages, a usage that, with only a few alterations, established the form of the present Roman rite. The two Offices may therefore be discussed together from the structural point of view. Differences between the two and deviations from present practice will be pointed out in considering the formal arrangement of the individual Hours. The complete sequence of items in each Office is given in Appendix I, which also contains the rubrics (generally translated) indicating items that are either to be taken from the Common of the Saints or to be repeated from a previous Hour. Incipits of poetic texts include the complete first verse, while for prose the first few words are followed by three dots. Where the original itself has only an incipit, as for the Psalms, it has been followed exactly, except for the resolution of abbreviations. It should be noted here that, with rare exceptions, poetic texts are provided for all items destined to be set to music. Lessons, chapters, and prayers, on the other hand, constitute the important prose texts without music that are given in full in the manuscript. (These last remarks apply only to the actual Offices, not to the Mass in honor of St. Hylarion, which, because of its special nature, will be considered separately.)

VESPERS

In the Office of St. Hylarion, Vespers I includes five antiphons (with their Psalm incipits), chapter, great responsory, hymn, and the antiphon *ad Magnificat*. The versicle following the hymn is not specified, but a rubric indicates that versicles and short responds for both day and night Hours are to be taken from the Common of "simple confessors" (f. 2v). First Vespers in the Office of St. Anne, on the other hand, has no opening antiphons but begins directly with the chapter, from which point it is identical in structure with the Vespers for Hylarion.

The Second Vesper services in both Offices are complete but differ from each other in the number of previously used items to be repeated. For St. Hylarion there is a new set of five antiphons as well as a new antiphon *ad Magnificat*, but Psalms, chapter, hymn, and versicle are to be taken from First Vespers. No mention is made of a great responsory, but presumably it too would be repeated from Vespers I. In Second Vespers for St. Anne, the only new text (and music) is the antiphon for the Magnificat. A rubric (f. 19) directs that the antiphons of Lauds are to be used with Psalms from the Common of Virgins, while the remaining items are indicated by text incipits. Chapter, hymn, and versicle are those of First Vespers, but the responsory is the sixth in Matins. This shift is possible because the *Gloria patri*, which closes the Vespers responsories, is also used at the end of Nocturn responsories 3, 6, and 9.

Two aspects of these Vespers services call for brief comment: the disparity in the number of antiphons, and the presence of great responsories. The Hylarion Office is unusual in having two complete sets of Vesper antiphons as well as five antiphons for Lauds. A similar situation exists in some of the rhymed *historiae* published in the *Analecta Hymnica*, but much more frequently Vespers II has only the antiphon *ad Magnificat*. There are even some cases in which only this antiphon is given in both Vespers, with a complete set of five antiphons appearing nowhere except in Lauds. Unfortunately, the lack of rubrics in AH and the policy of printing only the poetic texts make the complete liturgical form of these *historiae* impossible to re-establish. It may be assumed, however, that for Vespers II, the antiphons of Vespers I or of Lauds were to be repeated, and where only Lauds has a complete set of five antiphons, they would also serve for both Vesper services. All of these situations, be it noted, still exist in the present liturgy. For Ascension (*LU*, pp. 844 ff.), the antiphons for Vespers II also serve for Vespers I and Lauds. Corpus Christi (*LU*, pp. 917 ff.) uses the same antiphons for both Vespers but has a different set for Lauds. For the Nativity of St. John the Baptist (*LU*, pp. 1496 ff.), on the other hand, two sets of antiphons are assigned differently: one for Vespers I and the other for Lauds and Vespers II. Finally, for the Nativity of Our Lord (*LU*, pp. 364 ff.), each of the three services is provided with its own set of five antiphons. In the Cypriot Office of St. Anne, then, the repetition in Second Vespers of the antiphons for

Lauds is not without precedent and need occasion no surprise. What is unusual in this Office is that Vespers I has neither antiphons with Psalm incipits nor any indication that they are to be supplied from another source. A possible explanation of this anomaly will be given later, in considering the reappearance of the St. Anne Office in a printed breviary of 1497.

The second aspect of the Vesper services in both Offices that calls for comment is the presence of a great responsory. Such a responsory following the chapter, although not a part of the present Vesper service, was quite common even in late medieval times. Pierre Batifol notes that the Rule of St. Benedict "sets down a lesson at this point, but does not call it 'short' and attaches to it a respond, hymn, and versicle", and he queries whether this may represent an old Roman custom. According to the translator's note it probably does, because "so many of the medieval breviaries, Dominican, Sarum, etc., have a respond after the short lesson at Vespers. It is unlikely that they borrowed it from the Benedictines" [1]. Bonniwell, citing Amalarius as his authority, shows that a respond after the chapter at Vespers actually was a part of the old Roman Office. He says, moreover, that the practice persisted in Rome at least until the middle of the 12th century, and "the Dominicans elected to retain the ancient custom" [2]. From the fairly common appearance of Vesper responsories in the rhymed *historiae* published in *AH*, it would seem that the practice persisted, if not in Rome, throughout much of the rest of Europe until long after the 12th century. And if Dreves is correct in saying that the Dominicans always sang the Vesper Psalms *sub una antiphona*, then they cannot have been the only ones who "elected to retain the ancient custom" [3]. Given the close association between the Dominicans and the Court of Cyprus, the inclusion of Vespers responsories in the Tu B Offices

1 Pierre Batifol, *History of the Roman Breviary*, trans. Atwell M. Y. Bayley from the 3rd French ed. (London, N.Y., etc.; Longmans, Green & Co., 1912), p. 73 and n. 4.

2 William R. Bonniwell, O.P., *A History of the Dominican Liturgy 1215-1945* (2d ed.; New York: Joseph F. Wagner, Inc., 1945), p. 133.

3 *Analecta Hymnica* V, 11. In this same volume, *historiae* having both five antiphons and a responsory may be seen on pp. 42, 51, 53, 57, and 59 among others. *De Corona Spinea* (No. 10, p. 42) comes from a printed breviary of 1519.

may have been the result of their influence [4]. However, the presence of five antiphons rather than one makes it much more probable that these Offices follow traditional patterns that were still widely used and were by no means restricted to a single religious order.

MATINS

The remaining Hours of the two Offices may be more briefly dealt with, since they are nearly identical, not only with each other but also with the forms in present use. In both of the Tu B Offices, the invitatory of Matins follows immediately after the antiphon *ad Magnificat* of First Vespers. Only the chant itself is identified, although the beginning of all the other Hours is indicated by rubric. After the *Venite exultemus* (Ps 94), for which no more than the intonation is given, a hymn in each Office precedes the beginning of the Nocturns.

All of the Nocturns follow the standard, non-monastic form of three antiphons (with their psalms) and three lessons, each followed by a great responsory. In each Office, then, a total of nine antiphons and nine responsories constitutes the poetic and musical portion of the three Nocturns. The versicles that separate antiphons and psalms from the lessons and responsories are not indicated in the Hylarion Office, where they would presumably be drawn from the Common of Confessors as specified in the rubric of First Vespers. In the St. Anne Office, however, the text incipit of the versicle is given after the third antiphon of each Nocturn, and in Nocturn 2, even the musical formula is written out (f. 16). The only other difference between the two Offices occurs at the end of Nocturn 3, where the Hylarion Office has a rubric indicating performance of the *Te Deum* immediately after the ninth responsory. This indication is missing in the Office of St. Anne, but presumably omission of the *Te Deum* itself is not implied. (It is called for in the printed version of this Office to be discussed below.) The few differences between the two Matin services thus prove to be a matter of the completeness with which traditional elements are specified rather than variations in the essential structure.

The present order of Matins, at least in the Roman rite, exhibits only

[4] Cf., R. Hoppin, *Cypriot-French Repertory* II, xiv.

one significant departure from the structure of the Offices in Tu B. The ninth responsory has now been suppressed, with the result that the *Te Deum* follows immediately after Lesson IX. According to Bonniwell, retention of the ninth responsory is characteristic of Dominican services. Speaking of a "Dominican office-book compiled before Humbert's revision" (completed in 1256), he says: "In the third nocturn, we find a response given for the ninth lesson even though the *Te Deum* followed, a custom continued to the present day in the Order" [5]. That the custom was by no means confined to the Dominican Order, even as late as the early 16th century, may be inferred from the rhymed Offices published in *AH*, the great majority of which have three responsories for Nocturn 3. Again we must assume that, rather than proving Dominican influence, the presence of a ninth responsory in the Tu B Offices merely reflects the persistence of tradition in the early years of the 15th century.

LAUDS AND THE DIURNAL HOURS

In both Offices the structure of Lauds differs in no way from present usage. Five antiphons, with their psalms, are followed by a chapter, an antiphon *ad Benedictus*, and a prayer, the chapter and prayer being repeated from First Vespers. In the Hylarion Office, the service of Lauds is introduced by the rubric *In laudibus et pro horas diei* (f. 8), but there is no further indication of any material for the Little Hours. The Office of St. Anne, on the other hand, contains the chapters for Terce, Sext, and None and the direction to use the *responsoria* (short) from the Common of Virgins (f. 18v). However, there is no indication of the antiphons to be used for these Little Hours. On the basis of both present practice and the rubric in the Hylarion Office, we may assume that each of the four Little Hours would use one of the antiphons of Lauds, probably in the order 1, 2, 3, and 5. (Now, at least, antiphon 4, for the Canticle of the Three Children, is apparently regarded as the one most suitably omitted) [6].

Following Lauds, the Office of St. Hylarion contains a complete Mass to be described later. There is no indication of a Mass for the Office of St. Anne, which proceeds directly from the diurnal Hours to Second

5 Bonniwell, *op. cit.*, p. 38.

6 Cf. the Offices of Corpus Christi (LU, pp. 942 ff.) and the Nativity of Our Lord (LU, pp. 403, 407, and 411).

Vespers. The form of this service, with which both Offices close, has already been discussed.

It is clear that the authors of the Tu B Offices were following two basic traditions, with both of which they were thoroughly familiar: the tradition of the rhymed *historia* providing poetic texts for antiphons, invitatory, and responsories; and the much older tradition establishing the liturgical structure of the Offices as a whole. No formal deviations exist to be attributed to the insular origin of the Cypriot Offices. On the contrary, they are not only liturgically correct, but they reproduce in every detail the patterns to be observed in 14th- and 15th-century rhymed *historiae* from western Europe. We need not be surprised, then, to discover the same respect for tradition in the musical settings of the texts. Before discussing the music, however, we must note the unexpected discovery of a textual concordance for the Office of St. Anne.

THE OFFICE OF ST. ANNE IN TU B AND OD

Up to the present time, not a single concordance for the Tu B repertory, either textual or musical, was known to exist. It thus becomes a matter of considerable interest that the Office of St. Anne reappears in a breviary of the Use of Odense, printed in Lübeck in 1497. The surprising fact that we now have two versions, one coming from Cyprus in the early years of the 15th century and the other from Denmark some eighty years later, makes a rather detailed comparison of the two well worth while.

Anything more than a brief description of the Odense Breviary would serve no useful purpose here. Apparently the only extant copy is now in the Royal Library of Copenhagen [7]. It is in almost perfect condition, although there seem to be a few missing pages and some that are duplicated. There is now no title page, but the final paragraph (f. 465) establishes the book's origin and date of publication: *More othinensis cathedre qui psallere tentant / Canonicas horas docmata nostra legant / Solvere quaque die debita vota potes / Per Lucam Brandis opulenta Lubeck impressus / Necnon Matheo suo fratri administrante. Anno domini. Mccccxcvii.*

The original pagination is not very useful, since only the first and

[7] Kgl. Bibl., Da. afd. L.N. 30. Cf., *Gesamt Katalog der Wiegendrucke* (Leipzig, 1932), Band 5, Nr. 5419.

third recto pages in each group of eight have been numbered (Ai, Aii, Bi, Bii; etc.). However, the recto pages have been numbered consecutively by two later hands. Both foliations are in the upper right-hand corner, with the one that is higher and farther to the right being first one, then two, numbers ahead of the other. For page references to the Odense Breviary (Od) I have used this higher — in two senses — foliation, primarily because it is more clearly visible in the microfilm.

The *historia* of St. Anne — it is so designated in the calendar of Od — begins on f. 284v. It is a complete Office, from Vespers I to Vespers II, but of course, and unfortunately, only the texts are given. The rhymed portions of this Office, but not including the hymns, were published in the first volume of *Analecta Hymnica* devoted to rhymed *historiae* [8]. It is just these portions, as it happens, that are common to both the Tu B and Od versions. However, the correspondence might easily have gone unrecognized — had anyone previously checked the *Analecta Hymnica* — because the Od Office is provided with an entirely different First Vespers. Once it had been discovered that the remaining Hours of the two rhymed *historiae* were identical, or nearly so, it became imperative to compare the entire text of the Odense Office with the earlier version from Cyprus. Therefore, although almost all of the texts common to both versions are to be found in *AH*, the following discussion is based primarily on the complete text of the Office as it appears in the Odense Breviary.

First Vespers in Od is a complete service, with five antiphons, chapter, short respond, hymn, versicle, antiphon *ad Magnificat*, and collect. Of all these texts, only the chapter is the same as in Tu B. (No more than the incipit is given in Od.) Even the poetic antiphon *ad Magnificat* of Tu B is not used in Od. It would seem that, in order to change the fragmentary First Vespers of Tu B into a complete service, another source had been tapped for all of the poetic texts. They do, in fact, appear in other breviaries as Vespers I of an entirely different *historia* of St. Anne [9].

Correspondence between the two Offices, then, begins with the invitatory and continues through the nine antiphons of Nocturns and

8 *AH* V, 115. The Odense Breviary is the only source of this *historia* listed by Dreves (p. 117).

9 Cf., *AH* V, 109, the notes to *historia* No. 34. Three of the sources for this *historia* have "in 1. Vesp. alles wie im Brevier von Odensee".

the five antiphons of Lauds. All of these texts are identical and appear in the same order in both Offices. The prose antiphon *ad Benedictus* in Tu B is replaced by a poetic text but reappears in Od as the antiphon *ad Magnificat* for Vespers II. Both Offices specify that the antiphons of Lauds are to be used for Second Vespers, and Od also indicates their use for the daily Hours as well (f. 286v). This justifies the earlier assumption that, despite the lack of any indication in the Tu B Office, the antiphons of Lauds were to be used for the daily Hours.

The greatest divergence between the two Offices, in their rhymed portions, at least, occurs in the great responsories. The Use of Odense apparently called for no more than a short respond after the chapter of Vespers. Hence the Office of St. Anne in Od contains only the nine Nocturn responsories. With one exception, however, they are taken from the Tu B Office, as may be seen in Table 1. In Od the basic order of the Tu B responsories is followed, but Resp. 3 and 4 are interchanged, a new text is introduced for Resp. 6, and the Tu B responsory of Vespers I becomes Resp. 8. Thus one responsory in Od is not found in Tu B, while two of the latter's responsories are omitted from the Od Office. These changes in the responsory texts of the later Office would seem to have been occasioned both by the suppression of the Vesper responsory and by the completely different lessons in Od. This is especially clear in the case of Lesson 7 in Od, in which the *Liber generationis Jesu Christi* according to Matthew is followed by a commentary of St. Jerome: *In Ysiaa legimus generacionem eius* . . . Obviously, Resp. 6 in Tu B, *Genealogia Christi,* is more appropriate after this lesson and accordingly becomes Resp. 7 in Od. Such rearrangement of the responsory texts follows naturally on their liturgical function as complements to the lessons. The antiphons, on the other hand, could be, and were, used as they stood, as they were associated with the fixed texts of psalms and canticles.

Table 1

Correspondence of Responsories in Od and Tu B

Od		Tu B
Resp. 1	=	Resp. 1
Resp. 2	=	Resp. 2
Resp. 3	=	Resp. 4
Resp. 4	=	Resp. 3
Resp. 5	=	Resp. 5
Resp. 6		Not in Tu B
Resp. 7	=	Resp. 6
Resp. 8	=	Resp. of Vespers I
Resp. 9	=	Resp. 7

Textual variants in the poetry common to Tu B and Od are relatively slight and need not be studied in detail. In a few cases these variants result from unnoted "corrections" in Dreves' printed edition. In Ant. 3 of Nocturn 2, for example, Dreves has *regiam* for the last word of the second line. In both Tu B and Od, however, the word is *virginem*, which at least provides a better rhyme for *celibem*. Similarly in Resp. 3 (4 in Od), the last line reads *et in terris homines* in both sources, but Dreves has corrected it to *et in terra homines*. On the other hand, the text of Od sometimes removes faulty prosody or restores rhymes that are absent from the Tu B version. In Ant. 2 of Nocturn 1, the *patriarchali* of Tu B becomes *patriarcharum* to rhyme with *regum*, which, however, is *regnum* in Od. Dreves' correction here has removed the variant between the two versions. In this same antiphon, the probably incorrect repetition of *originem* at the ends of lines 2 and 4 in Tu B is changed in Od by the substitution of *propaginem* in line 4. Examples of corrected prosody may be seen in the first two Nocturn responsories. The final line of Resp. 1, which has only six syllables in Tu B (*virgo puerpera*), is changed in Od to *et vite puerpera* to produce a normal 7-syllable line. The 6-syllable lines (2 and 4) in Resp. 2 are similarly changed in Od to lines of seven syllables. Presumably, these variants could serve as an excuse for postulating a third, "original" version, antedating both Od and Tu B. This easy way out, however, would only deepen our ignorance. That the variants to be found in Od represent corrections and adaptations of the Tu B Office seems a much more profitable, and probable, assumption.

Apart from the poetic texts and the one prose antiphon, the Offices in Tu B and Od show very little correspondence. As has been indicated above, the nine lessons for Nocturns, the longest prose texts, are entirely different. Furthermore, none of the hymns in Tu B reappears in the Od Office. The prayers are also different, but other short texts, chapters, versicles and short responds, for the most part are the same. This is not surprising, since it is just these texts that are taken from the Common of Virgins or of Holy Women. Indeed, many of the same versicles and responds appear in both of these Commons and in the Common of the Feast of the Virgin Mary as well. That the Tu B and Od Offices of St. Anne generally correspond in their use of these shorter texts has no significance beyond showing that they both adhere to the liturgical traditions of the western Church.

One peculiarity in the Odense Breviary may explain the incomplete First Vespers of the Tu B Office. A calendar prefixed to the breviary (f. 1-6v) lists all the feast days and indicates the nature of the special texts for each [10]. For July 26, the present Feast of St. Anne, the calendar reads *Translatio Anne et Christofori Collecta.* However, in the breviary itself the nine lessons for St. James on July 25 are followed by a *historia* of St. Martha on July 27 (now the 29th), and only a collect for the *memoria* of St. Christopher is to be found in Vespers I of the St. James Office (f. 364v). Returning to the calendar, we find that the *historia* of St. Anne is listed for December 9, the day following the Feast of the Immaculate Conception, and this is where it occurs in the breviary [11]. After the antiphon *ad Magnificat* for Vespers II of the Immaculate Conception, there comes the following suggestive rubric: *Post benedicamus memoria de sancta Anna ubi non fuerit patrocinium. Sed si fuerit patrocinium tunc sequuntur vespere cum quinque antiphonis per omnia laudate* (f. 284v). The complete Office of St. Anne then follows. The implication of the rubric would seem to be that where there was no patronage, Vespers I of the St. Anne Office

[10] The common notations indicate a collect (for a simple commemoration or *memoria*), three lessons, nine lessons, or a *historia.*

[11] The calendar reads as follows

		[Decembris]	
vi	[ante idus]	Conceptionis Marie	Histo.
v		Anne matris Marie	Histo.

would be omitted. Where there was patronage, however, two complete Vesper services would apparently be performed in succession. Additional support for this interpretation is the lack of any reference to Compline, customarily found in Od, at the end of the Office of the Immaculate Conception. Instead, Vespers I of the St. Anne Office is followed by the rubric *Completorium sicut in priori nocte cum suffragiis ex Adventu.* At the close of the St. Anne Office, another reference to Compline says simply *Completorium ex Adventu.*

The performance of two complete Vesper services in succession would seem to be an abnormal and illogical situation, since presumably the same psalms would be sung for both. Yet the assumption that the Office in Tu B was also intended for use on December 9, following the Immaculate Conception, provides a plausible explanation for the incomplete state of its First Vespers. The service as it exists in Tu B could be sung either as an extended *memoria* following the Vespers of the preceding feast, or as a replacement for the corresponding parts of those Vespers. The latter solution seems the more likely, and, indeed, it is the procedure prescribed in the present *Rubricae generales Breviarii* when Second and First Vespers of two *Festa Duplici* fall on the same day [12]. Vespers I of the Cypriot Office of St. Anne, then, would not be incomplete but would contain all of the texts, beginning with the chapter, that were needed for use with the concurrent Vespers II of the Immaculate Conception.

To summarize the most important relationships between the two Offices, we may recall that twenty-four texts with musical settings in Tu B reappear in the Odense breviary: the invitatory, nine antiphons of Nocturns , five antiphons of Lauds, eight responsories, and the prose antiphon *ad Benedictus* in Tu B that is used *ad Magnificat* in Od. Thus, with the exception of Vespers I, the Odense Office has taken over almost intact the rhymed *historia* of St. Anne from the earlier Cypriot source. Whether the music as well as the texts travelled to Denmark remains an unanswered question. Unfortunately, no Odense antiphonaries of the period are known to have survived, and the probability of finding the Office in another

12 *Duplici ergo in secundis Vesperis concurrente cum alio sequenti Duplici in primis, si utraque sint ejusdem solemnitatis, regulariter a Capitulo fit de sequenti cum Commemoratione praecedentis. Breviarium Romanum* (New York; Benzinger Brothers, Inc., 1946), p. xxxiv (of separate pamphlet, *Bullae, Tabellae, Rubricae generales . . .*).

musical source seems extremely remote. For the present we can only record the circumstance — and curious enough it is — that a Danish breviary provides the only known concordance for any part of the Cypriot repertory [13].

[13] The Odense breviary has another equally interesting and mysterious connection with musical history. According to Bukofzer, it is the only known source containing the text in honor of St. Alban that accompanies the tenor of Dunstable's motet *Albanus roseo — Quoque ferendus — Albanus domini laudans*. Cf. John Dunstable, *Complete Works*, ed. M. Bukofzer (*Musica Britannica* VIII; London, 1953), No. 23, p. 58; and Note on p. 174.

MODAL ORDER IN THE PLAINCHANT REPERTORY

The remainder of the present Commentary will be devoted in large part to a consideration of the musical forms and styles to be found in the Offices and Mass cycles in Tu B. Before the individual types of chant are dealt with, however, some attention must be paid to the organization of groups of chants by means of an ordered succession of modes. Such organization, which has already been noted in the series of motets based on the Great Antiphons for Advent [1], proves to be a striking characteristic of the Cypriot plainchant repertory.

The Mass cycles will be discussed later, but it may be noted here that the six cycles, each of which remains in one mode throughout, are arranged in an ascending modal order. Cycles 1, 2, and 3 are all in mode 1; cycle 4 is in mode 2; and cycles 5 and 6 are in modes 5 and 6 respectively. Arrangements of this sort obviously have no musical, *i.e.*, auditory, significance whatsoever. Rather, they are ever-recurrent witnesses to man's inherent passion for intellectual order. That passion is equally in evidence in the Offices of Tu B, although here one may question whether intellectual order does not also become, at least in some instances, an audible musical phenomenon.

In Table 2 are listed the modes of the chants in three Offices: St. Hylarion and St. Anne from Tu B, and, for purposes of comparison, Corpus Christi (*LU*, pp. 917 ff.). That the Office of St. Hylarion presents the most complex and variously organized modal successions is immediately apparent. After the eight chants of Vespers I have presented all of the modes in succession from 1 to 8, the remaining Hours adopt other patterns of modal order. The antiphons and responsories of Nocturns seem to be rather more loosely organized, although certain obvious groupings appear within the units of three chants. Moreover, there is a gradual progression to mode 8 in Resp. 6, with another arrival at mode 8 and a return to mode 1 in the last three responsories. It can scarcely be by chance that, of the eighteen Nocturn chants, four are in mode 1, with two in each of the other

[1] Cf. CMM 21, II, v; Nos. 23-30.

seven modes. Lauds and Vespers II are more systematically arranged and present ingenious variations on the idea of modal succession. In Lauds, the modes appear in reverse order within the *manierae,* which progress forward, however, from *protus* to *tetrardus, deuterus* being skipped. Both procedures are reversed in Vespers II. The modes are in normal order within the *manieriae,* and the progression is now from *tetrardus* to *protus.* Unfortunately, the liturgical necessity of repeating the responsory and hymn from Vespers I made this modal order impossible to maintain throughout. However, the mode of the final antiphon *ad Mag.* (Mode 2) provides the correct ending to the series projected by the first five antiphons.

The same principles are followed in the Office of St. Anne, although here the modal successions are less systematically carried out. Only in the first nine chants of Nocturns do we find a patterned progression through the modes from 1 to 8. The less complicated organization of the St. Anne Office is due in part to the presence of only one set of five antiphons, but it also reflects the greater simplicity that differentiates that Office as a whole from the Office of St. Hylarion.

Table 2

Modal Succession in Office Chants

Hours	Chants		Modes *	
		Hylarion	Anne	Corpus Christi
Vespers I	Ant. 1	1	—	(1)
	Ant. 2	2	—	(2)
	Ant. 3	3	—	(3)
	Ant. 4	4	—	(4)
	Ant. 5	5	—	(5)
	Resp.	6	5	—
	Hymn	7	6	(3)
	Ant. ad Mag.	8	1	6
Matins	Invit.	4	4	4
	Hymn	5	3	4
Noct. 1	Ant. 1	1	1	1
	Ant. 2	1	3	2
	Ant. 3	1	5	3
	Resp. 1	2	2	1
	Resp. 2	4	4	2
	Resp. 3	5	6	3

* Numbers in parentheses indicate chants repeated from another Hour.

Noct. 2	Ant. 4	2	6	4
	Ant. 5	4	7	5
	Ant. 6	6	8	6
	Resp. 4	3	1	5
	Resp. 5	7	3	6
	Resp. 6	8	7	7
Noct. 3	Ant. 7	3	5	7
	Ant. 8	5	7	8
	Ant. 9	7	4	6
	Resp. 7	8	5	7
	Resp. 8	6	6	8
	Resp. 9	1	1	—
Lauds	Ant. 1	2	1	1
	Ant. 2	1	2	2
	Ant. 3	6	3	3
	Ant. 4	5	5	4
	Ant. 5	8	6	5
	Hymn	7	1	8
	Ant. ad Bened.	1	1	1
Vespers II	Ant. 1	7	(1)	1
	Ant. 2	8	(2)	2
	Ant. 3	5	(3)	3
	Ant. 4	6	(5)	4
	Ant. 5	3	(6)	5
	Resp.	(6)	(7)	—
	Hymn	(7)	(6)	3
	Ant. ad Mag.	2	5	5

Attention must be called to one more aspect of the overall modal organization. A number of Hours in both Offices seem to achieve tonal unity through the use of mode 1 (or 2) for the opening and closing chants. Indeed, in the Office of St. Hylarion the emphasis on the *protus* tonality as both a starting point and a final goal is so striking that it might well be called an Office in D. To what extent this tonal unity reflects the conscious application of a musical concept is impossible to say. Certainly it is in part merely the result of playing with numbers, and the tonal unity of services occurring at intervals over a period of twenty-four hours could only be an intellectual, not an audible, phenomenon. Yet whatever may have been its cause, this unity does, in effect, exist, both in the individual Hours and in the complete Office of St. Hilarion. That the Office of Corpus Christi shows a similar organization only for Lauds may be taken as a preliminary indication that the consistent achievement of tonal unity was a contribution of the Cypriot composers or of the period in which they lived. The tonally unified Mass cycle, after all, was primarily a development of the 15th century. We need not be surprised, therefore, to find a related concept being applied to the chants of the Offices.

Wherever the concept of tonal unity may have originated, the practice of arranging the Office chants in a modal succession was by no means an innovation of the Cypriot composers. On the contrary, their arrangement of the Tu B Offices is but one more, and very strong, indication of how closely they adhered to the traditions of European plainchant. A century and a half earlier the chants for the Office of Corpus Christi had been disposed in the numerical order of the modes. (See Table 2). This Feast, for which St. Thomas Aquinas wrote the Office, was established for the Universal Church in 1264. Perhaps it is not too farfetched to regard the notably simpler and more straightforward modal successions in this Office as representative of 13th-century ideals in contrast to the late Gothic complexities of the St. Hylarion Office.

Going back to the 12th century, we find consistent and extended modal successions throughout the Office of St. James from Santiago de Compostela. These successions, which are shown in Table 3, need no further comment, except, perhaps, with regard to the arrangement of Nocturns.

Table 3

Modal Arrangement of Chants in the Office of St. James

Hour	Chants	Modes
Lauds of Vigil	5 Ant. & Ant. ad Bened.	1 2 3 4 5 & 8
Vespers I	5 Ant. & Ant. ad Mag.	1 2 3 4 5 & 8
Nocturns	13 Ant.	1 2 3 4 5 6 7 8 1 2 3 4 5
	12 Resp.	1 2 3 4 5 6 7 8 1 8 8 1
Lauds	5 Ant. & Ant. ad Bened.	1 2 3 4 5 & 1
Vespers II	Ant. of Lauds & Ant. ad Mag.	(1 2 3 4 5) & 3

The Office of St. James being monastic, there are thirteen antiphons and twelve responsories for the three Nocturns. In the manuscript source these chants are written in two separate groups, each having the independent modal series shown in Table 3. Liturgical performance, however, would distribute the antiphons six, six, and one (*ad cantica*) and the responsories in three groups of four. The two modal series would thus appear in the following alternation:

Table 4

		Antiphons	Responsories
Nocturn 1.	Modes:	1 2 3 4 5 6	1 2 3 4
Nocturn 2.	Modes:	7 8 1 2 3 4	5 6 7 8
Nocturn 3.	Modes:	5	1 8 8 1

Peter Wagner, whose discussion of modal arrangement in the St. James Office provided the basis for the foregoing summary, makes it clear that here, too, following the numerical order of the modes was not an innovation [2]. Wagner found the procedure first authenticated in the 10th-century Trinity Office, and shortly thereafter it was followed whenever a new Office needed music. It is Wagner's view that no liturgical or artistic purpose for such modal ordering can be adduced, and he calls it a *Spielerei* comparable to Bach's arrangement of the Well-Tempered Clavier [3]. This is especially interesting when we recall Manfred Bukofzer's discussion of "inaudible order" in the Baroque era, particularly in the works of Bach, whose ordering of the canons in the *Goldberg Variations* Bukofzer ascribes to "intellectual playfulness" [4].

It is extremely difficult to decide when such playfulness begins to serve an artistic purpose. To put it another way, the point at which an intellectual order becomes an audible phenomenon can never be exactly determined. Not only will the point differ for different individuals, but it will vary for one individual according to the development of his musical knowledge and sensitivity. It seems almost inconceivable, however, that all of the modal series in medieval Offices should have passed unperceived by the musically sophisticated. Be that as it may, these Offices make it abundantly clear that the imposition of an intellectual order upon a group of related pieces was not peculiar to the Baroque era. It seems not to have been generally realized, or at least it has been rarely stated, that Baroque composers were merely following a tradition that can be documented in almost the earliest surviving collections of western music. The Offices in

2 Peter Wagner, *Die Gesänge der Jakobusliturgie zu Santiago de Compostela aus dem sog. Codex Calixtinus* (Freiburg, 1931), pp. 155 ff.

3 *Ibid.*, p. 159 & n. 3. Cf. also P. Wagner, *Einführung in die gregorianischen Melodien*, III, 318. The Vesper antiphons of the Trinity Office may be seen in *LU*, p. 914.

4 Manfred Bukofzer, *Music in the Baroque Era* (New York, 1947), p. 368.

Tu B, particularly that of St. Hylarion, quite obviously acknowledge and continue this tradition, even then centuries old. They go beyond the simple modal successions of earlier Offices, however, to more intricate and more ingenious orders, by means of which the tradition itself is expanded and enriched.

LITURGICAL RECITATIVE

An examination of the various types of chant represented in the Tu B repertory may well begin with what Willi Apel has called "liturgical recitative" [1]. Indications for the performance of psalms and canticles constitute a seemingly insignificant part of this total repertory. Brief as they are, however, these indications provide convincing evidence that Cypriot plainchant closely adhered to the traditional practices of western Europe.

The simplest forms of recitative, for lessons and prayers, are not indicated at all, and one can only assume that the traditional formulas were used. The same assumption must be made for versicles and short responds, which, if they are specified at all, are normally identified only by the text incipit. In one case, however, in Nocturn 2 of the Office of St. Anne (f. 16), the musical formula for the versicle is written out. As may be seen in Ex. 1, this formula is exceptional only in its slight elaboration of the final notes. Whether this variant was in common usage or was of purely local origin remains to be determined. According to Wagner, Ex. 1c, one of several settings in a 15th-century manuscript, follows the older practice of using *a* for a reciting tone. In late medieval times, however, reciting tones on *c* or *f*, as in Ex. 1d, were commonly the rule[2].

Example 1
Versicle Tones

a. Tu B, f. 16

b. LU, p. 118

c. Wagner, Einf. III, 31.

d. Ibid., p. 33.

1 W. Apel, *Gregorian Chant* (Bloomington, 1958), pp. 201 ff.

2 P. Wagner, *Einführung in die gregorianischen Melodien*, III, 31 ff.

Complete formulas for chanting psalms and canticles are, of course, not to be found in the Hylarion and Anne Offices. As in regular antiphonaries, each antiphon is normally followed only by one of the terminations for the tone to be used. These terminations are accompanied by either a text incipit or the vowels EVOVAE of the *seculorum amen.* Intonations for the tones are not generally given, although they do appear in four instances, three of which are for the Magnificat. In the Office of St. Anne, the Magnificat intonations for Tones 1 and 5 are given in Vespers I and II respectively (f. 14v and 19). Since these intonations are identical with those of the normal psalm tones, there seems to be no reason for their inclusion except, perhaps, as a reminder that they were to be sung with each verse. In Vespers II for Hylarion, the intonation for Tone 2 follows the termination and is written a third too low (f. 13). Apart from the latter singularity, which must be an error, the seeming afterthought might be accounted for by the difference between the Magnificat and psalm tone intonations [3]. However, in Vespers I for Hylarion, only the termination is given for the Magnificat in Tone 8, although this tone also has a more elaborate intonation than the normal psalm tone. In neither Office, it may be noted, is there an intonation for the Benedictus at Lauds, which is in Tone 1 in both instances. The absence of intonations for some canticles argues against any strong reason for their occasional presence, and it surely must have been mere caprice that led the scribe to include the intonation of Tone 5 after the third antiphon of Nocturn 1 in the Office of St. Anne (f. 15). Whatever may have been the reasons, if any, behind the appearance of these few intonations, they are now received with gratitude as a first indication that the forms of western psalmody were known and used in the Cypriot service. A second and much stronger indication is to be found in the terminations that, as has been indicated, invariably follow the antiphons for psalms and canticles.

Long ago Peter Wagner remarked that writing the thousand-year history of the *differentiae* from Aurelian of Réomé to the *Editio vaticana*

[3] The intonation as given in Tu B has only one note (*d*) for the second syllable instead of the clivis of the Vatican Edition (LU, pp. 208 and 214). It corresponds exactly, however, with the formula given by Wagner in his "Initia der Canticapsalmodie", *Einführung*, III, 118.

would be a profitable undertaking [4]. Even less than in his monumental study can such a project be thought of here. Yet a brief look at the terminations to be found in Tu B will provide something more than a footnote to that history.

All of the termination formulas from the Hylarion and Anne Offices are assembled in Table 4, with the tone and final note of each providing the identifying designation [5]. The presence or absence of these terminations in other sources, both practical and theoretical, has been indicated under Concordances in Table 4. The identification of these sources is as follows:

LU	*The Liber Usualis with Introduction and Rubrics in English*, (New York, 1956), pp. 113 ff
Luc	*Le Codex 601 de la Bibliothèque capitulaire de Lucques (XIIe siècle). Paléographie musicale* IX, *Tonale*, pp. 2 ff.
Worc	*Codex F. 160 de la Bibliothèque de la Cathédrale de Worcester (XIIIe siècle). Paléographie musicale* XII, 126 ff.
WagB	Paris, Bibl. Nat., n.a. 1235. Terminations from this French manuscript of the 12th century are given by Peter Wagner in column B of his tables. *Einführung in die Gregorianischen Melodien*, III, 132 ff.
Spec	Jacobus of Liège, *Speculum musicae* (Book VI). E. de Coussemaker, *Scriptorum de Musica Medii Aevi* (Paris, 1867), II, 326 ff.
Od	Tonary of Odo of Cluny. Coussemaker, *Scriptorum* II, 117 ff.
UO	Ugolino of Orvieto, *Declaratio musicae disciplinae*, ed. Albert Seay. 3 vols. (Rome, 1959-62), I, 104 ff. Numbers in ( ) refer to musical examples in separate booklet.

Some explanation is needed to show how concordances in these sources are indicated in Table 4. A dash means that the termination is not found, while U indicates a unique ending for the particular tone. The designations of the Vatican edition have been used in the column headed LU. For the other practical sources the numbers are those of the compiled

[4] *Einführung*, III, 131.

[5] These designations are also given before antiphons in the alphabetical index of all the chants in Tu B (Appendix II). A subtlety in the Vatican edition, the reason for which escapes me, is the designation of some endings by the first note of a final podatus (Tone 4, ending A*), while in other cases the second note of the podatus is taken for the designation (Tone 3, ending a^2). In designating the terminations in Tu B, the actual final note has been used in every case.

Table 4

PSALM-TONE TERMINATIONS IN OFFICES OF TU B

Termination		Concordances						
		LU	Luc	Worc	WagB	Spec	Od	UO
1.D		D	6	2	8	2 p. 329	6	8 (103)
1.f	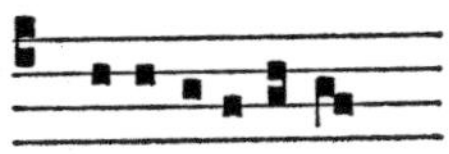	f	1	3	5	6	1	1 (67)
$1.f^2$		—	—	—	—	—	—	—
1.g		g	2	1	1	1	2?	2 (77)
$1.g^2$		—	5	—	—	—	3	3 (82)
1.a		a	4	7	4	3	7	4 (88)
2.D	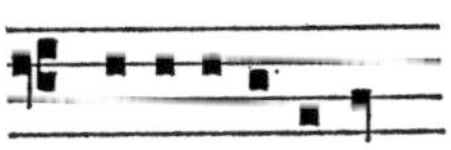	U	U	U	U	1 p. 340	U	U (120)
3.g		g	2	1	4	1 p. 343	2	2 (145)
$3.g^2$		—	—	—	—	p. 343	—	—
3.a		a^2	4	5	2	1 p. 344	3	3 (153)
3.b	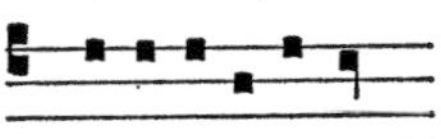	b	3	4	—	3 p. 344	—	—

Table 4 (cont.)

Termination		Concordances						
		LU	Luc	Worc	WagB	Spec	Od	UO
4.E		A	2	3	4	p. 347b	1?	1 (159)
4.f	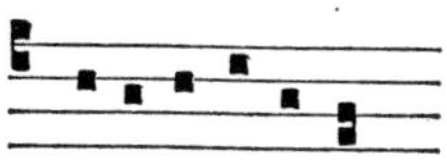	A*	1	5	6	p. 348	2	3 (203)
5.a	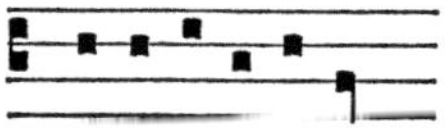	U	2	1	U	1 p. 352	1	U (211)
5.c	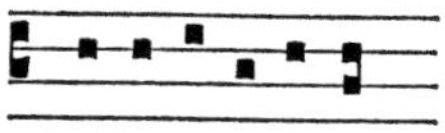	—	1	2	—	4?	2	—
6.F		U	U	U	U	p. 355	U	U (224)
6.F*		—	—	—	—	—	—	—
7.a		a	1	1	3	1 p. 358	1	6 (266)
7.c		c	2	2	1	p. 359?	2	5 (257)
7.c²		c²	5	4	2	p. 359	6	2 (244)
8.G	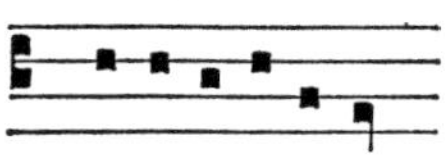	G	1	1	1	2 p. 362	1	1 (291)
8.c	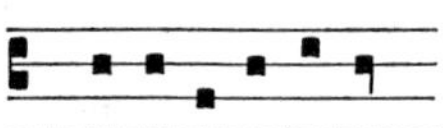	c	2	2	2	1	3	2 (328)

tonaries in the *Paléographie musicale* or Wagner's tables of terminations [6]. For the theoretical sources the numbering follows the order of the original where possible. With the *Speculum musicae,* however, it has sometimes been necessary to resort to page numbers as well. The *Speculum* is particularly important for the study of terminations, because it attempts to survey the varying practices that had existed or still did exist at the time the treatise was written. Thus for some tones there are several different sets of terminations. Unfortunately, the well-known unreliability of Coussemaker's edition makes one hesitate to use his musical examples as the basis for any firm conclusions [7]. After due allowance for possible errors, however, both theoretical and practical sources provide convincing evidence that liturgical recitative as performed in Cyprus was in almost complete conformity with established usage. A brief examination of the terminations for each tone will reveal the extent of that conformity. Even more important, however, are the questions it will pose for consideration by a future historian of the *differentiae.*

Tone 1. Four of the six terminations in Tu B appear in all seven of the concordances listed in Table 4. In these four, the only variant occurs in 1.D, where the penultimate syllable is sometimes sung to a single note, *g,* instead of the podatus *g-a* [8]. Of the less common terminations, 1.f² is in none of the concordances. It seems to be present, however, in the treatise published by Coussemaker under the title *Tractatus de Musica Plana cujusdam Carthusiensis Monachi* [9]. The formula given here has the same six notes as the ending in Tu B, but the last five are written as a ligature.

6 In column A of his tables, Wagner gives the terminations from the Lucca Ms. 601 that are also to be found in the Tonary in *PM* IX. Because Wagner uses a different numbering, and because there are minor discrepancies between the two, I have used the tonary accompanying the facsimile edition of the manuscript as the basis for the figures in the column headed Luc in Table 4.

7 Apart from errors of clefs, doubts are raised by repetitions of the same termination within a set and by discrepancies between the collected sets and the subsequent discussion and illustration of the individual terminations. Ending 7.c, for example, apears at the bottom of p. 359a, but is not found in any of the preceding examples of *differentiae* for Tone 7.

8 In WagB. In the Lucca Tonary, p. 2, the formula is given with the single note, but on p. 18 it has the podatus. LU, p. 113, gives both forms with the same designation.

9 CS II, 452b.

These notes would obviously have to be sung to the six syllables of EVOVAE, and this is not the only instance in the theoretical works when single notes of the terminations are combined into ligatures. Similar procedures may be observed occasionally in Tu B, particularly in the Office of St. Anne [10]. The other less common ending, 1.g², is apparently a variant of the LU ending 1.g², which has a torculus *g-a-g* for the final syllable instead of the clivis *a-g*. The relationship between the two is proved by the appearance of the Tu B version in the Toledo Ms with antiphons that, in Lucca 601, are normally followed by the LU ending [11].

Variants in the termination formulas such as those just cited raise a number of interesting questions. In Tone 1, for example, all of the terminations have the same first four notes, *a a g f*, both in Tu B and in the present Vatican edition. Yet some German sources substitute two-note ligatures, *a-g* and *g-f*, for the third and fourth notes [12]. These forms are also the first ones given by Jacobus in the *Speculum Musicae*. The forms with single notes, says Jacobus, were used in many churches *ut in Gallicanis et forsan Romanis* [13]. To what extent these variants and others like them actually did constitute regional chant dialects and the precise linguistic boundaries of such dialects remain to be determined. Another problem concerns the relative age of simpler and more elaborate versions. Preliminary evidence seems to indicate that the later Middle Ages saw both a simplification of the formulas and a reduction in their number. Full knowledge of this development, too, must await future investigations. No more appropriate place for raising these questions can be found than in connection with the *differentiae* of Tone 1. In Tu B, as in all the other sources, there are more endings for Tone 1, and those endings are themselves subject to greater variation, than for any other psalm tone of the plainchant repertory.

Tone 2. Tu B has a unique ending for Tone 2, as do all but one of the concordances. Only the *Speculum musicae* (p. 340) gives two alternate

10 E.g., on f. 18 the ending 1.D is written with no regard for the syllabic distribution of the text.

11 Cf. *PM* IX, pp. 17 and 24 of the Tonary.

12 Cf. Ludwig, *Einführung* III, 132, Column C.

13 *CS* II, 326 and 329.

endings, both of which end on D, however, and have the same final progression *c-d*. Within the unique ending one variant is sometimes found. The penultimate syllable may be sung to a podatus *c-d* instead of to the single note c [14]. Because the first folio is badly wrinkled, the termination after the antiphon *Gentes laudate dominus* gives the false impression of ending on *e*.

Tone 3. After Tone 1, Tone 3 exhibits the greatest variety in the number and character of its *differentiae*. Yet here again all but one of the Tu B endings prove to be the common property of western psalmody. The closely related 3.g and 3.a endings provide further examples of variants that interchange single notes and two-note ligatures. In every concordance, for example, the penultimate syllable of 3.a is set to a single *a* instead of to the *a-g* of the Tu B version. For ending 3.g, on the other hand, WagB replaces the penultimate *a* by a clivis *a-g*, while Spec has a single c instead of *c-b* above the third syllable. The customary presence of ending 3.b in the practical sources makes its absence from the treatises Od and UO somewhat surprising. It may well be the illegible ending that is omitted from Wagner's Table [15]. The Tu B ending $3.g^2$ appears in none of the concordances, although the same notes are to be found in Spec with a different placement of the ligature. Perhaps the similarity between this ending and 8.G led to its general rejection. Jacobus, in fact, speaks of the possibility of confusing Tones 3 and 8 and cites the 8.G ending [16]. The $3.g^2$ ending is used only once in Tu B for an antiphon that is clearly in the third mode (*Post labores fructiferos*, f. 13).

Tone 4. The two endings for this tone that are found in Tu B are fairly standard throughout the concordances. In LU, Worc and WagB, however, they are transposed up a fourth. Typical variants involving single notes versus two-note ligatures would seem to have been at least one of the factors determining which endings could or should be transposed. The 4.E ending in LU (*b-a g-f e*) is clearly just an ornamented version of the A ending (*e c a*), which equals 4.E in Tu B. Transposed to A, however,

14 In Luc and WagB.
15 *Einführung*, III, 134, n. 2.
16 *CS* II, 344b.

the 4.E ending of LU would lose its modal characteristics. A midpoint between these two versions is found in UO, where the second *differentia* is the same as the first (4.E in Tu B) but substitutes a clivis *b–a* for the single *b* on the antepenultimate syllable. The same substitution occurs in the UO version of the 4.f ending. Odo's first *differentia* is identical with 4.E (of Tu B) except that the final note is *f* instead of *e* [17]. This must surely be a mistake. The *Speculum* does not have ending 4.f but does have one that is identical except that the final podatus is *e–g* instead of *e–f*. This is a characteristic variant, but it may have been introduced here to avoid any suggestion of a tritone, which also vanishes, along with modal purity, when the formula is transposed up a fourth. A thorough study of the terminations of Tone 4 and their accompanying antiphons, it would seem, might be very revealing of performing musicians' attitudes toward modal identity and integrity.

Tone 5. Both theoretical and practical sources bear out Ugolino's statement that Tone 5 in earlier times was said to have two *differentiae* [18]. A century previously, Jacobus had said that, according to some, Tone 5 had only one *differentia*. He went on to report, however, that he had found as many as four in different tonaries [19]. Of these, the fourth is probably the 5.c ending of Tu B. The same seven notes are present, but the last two, instead of being a ligature, are written singly, at least as transcribed by Coussemaker. In any case, the 5.c ending is obviously formed by a characteristic substitution of a two-note ligature for the final single note of the common, and present, unique ending.

Tone 6. All sources give only one *differentia* for Tone 6. However, the single *differentia* cited by Jacobus in the *Speculum* is a more elaborate formula ending on *g* — possibly an error. In any case, Jacobus continues with a statement that the *antiqui* had another *differentia*, which proves to be the standard ending of all the other sources [20]. The second ending in

17 *CS* II, 126b.

18 Ugolini Urbevetanis *Declaratio Musicae Disciplinae*, I, 122.

19 *CS* II, 352a.

20 Sed antiqui unam aliam habebant differentiam hanc scilicet: (ending 6.F follows). CS II, 355b.

Tu B, 6.F*, if it is really intended as a variant, merely adds a liquescent sign to the second note. Liquescents are very rare in the Tu B repertory, but they are unmistakably indicated in two of the five examples of the Tone 6 ending [21]. There seems to be no rational explanation for this variant, which is, after all, but another instance when a two-note ligature — clivis or cephalicus — is substituted for a single note.

Tone 7. The three endings of Tone 7 in Tu B are standard formulas common to all sources. The only discrepancy to be noted occurs in ending 7.a, which is found but once in Tu B (f. 17). In place of the podatus *d-e*, all the concordances have separate notes, which produces the correct syllabic distribution. This would seem to be merely another instance when the scribe of Tu B has copied the notes correctly but has been unconcerned with the accommodation of those notes to the text [22].

Tone 8. Again the endings in Tu B are standard formulas that appear in all sources. The only variant in the seven concordances listed in Table 4 occurs in WagB, where the 8.G ending has a clivis *c-b* in place of the antepenultimate note.

That the psalm-tone terminations in Tu B are so obviously based on western traditions of psalmody is perhaps less surprising than the large number of different endings that are to be found in the two Offices. There are, after all, only forty-four antiphons in the Offices of St. Hylarion and St. Anne, yet no less than twenty-one different terminations are used [23]. Quite evidently the composer or composers of these Offices must have made a deliberate effort to introduce variety in the antiphonal psalmody by means of these different terminations. To put it another way, and perhaps more properly, variety was deliberately achieved through the use of different melodic formulas for the opening phrases of the antiphons, which naturally entailed the use of different terminations. The relationship

21 On f. 5v and 16. The ending with no liquescent occurs on f. 8v, 13, and 18. Other liquescents may be seen in the hymn *Gaudet chorus fidelium* and the antiphon *Hodie splendor eterni*, both on f. 18v.

22 Cf. the previous comment in the discussion of Tone 1.

23 This figure does not include ending 6.F*, which cannot be regarded as more than a variant of ending 6.F.

between antiphon beginnings and psalm-tone terminations is too complex to be dealt with here, although it will be considered briefly in discussing the Tu B antiphons. Meanwhile, a few more indications of traditional liturgical recitative in the Tu B Offices remain to be mentioned.

Both of the invitatories in Tu B are in mode 4, and, as is customary in medieval manuscripts, the formula for the invitatory psalm is indicated by the intonation rather than by the ending. The two different intonations (f. 3 and 14v) correspond with those that are designated as 4.E and 4.d in the Index of the Worcester Antiphonary [24]. Among the very few invitatories printed in the *Liber Usualis*, formula 4.E may be found on page 918, but formula 4.d does not occur. The latter would seem to be Wagner's fourth formula for Tone 4 [25]. The first six notes (all that appear in Tu B and Worc) are identical except for the opening podatus, which is *e-a* in Wagner but d-a in Worc and Tu B. Since the invitatory tones differ throughout, and not merely in their intonations and endings, the presence of nothing but the intonation makes it clear that both composers and performers knew the standard formulas. That no indications are given for the alternation of invitatory and psalm verses may be taken as evidence that they were equally well acquainted with the traditional method of performance.

The only other example of liturgical recitative in Tu B is to be found, not in the Offices, but in the Introit of the Mass for St. Hylarion (f. 9v). The verse of this Introit uses the standard form of Tone 5, with the only unusual feature being its partially tripartite division. Three phrases are clearly suggested in the musical setting, with a second intonation for phrases 2 and 3. Phrase 2, however, does not close with a normal mediant cadence. According to Willi Apel, the complete division into three phrases "is employed only for the *Gloria*, never for the verses" [26]. Whether the step toward a tripartite scheme taken in the Introit verse for St. Hylarion was a local aberration or whether it was following late medieval precedents has yet to be determined.

[24] *PM* XII, 176 f. Among other places in the facsmile, formula 4.E may be seen on pp. 33 and 38, formula 4.d on pp. 60 and 165.

[25] *Einführung* III, 178.

[26] W. Apel, *Gregorian Chant*, p. 229.

ANTIPHONS

Unlike liturgical recitative, in which prescribed psalms and canticles are sung to traditional musical formulas, the antiphons consist of poetic texts celebrating the particular saint in question. It is logical to assume, therefore, that the plainchant settings of these texts were also newly composed. Certainly in the case of the St. Hylarion Office, at least, both texts and melodies must have been written within a relatively short span of time. In the course of the following discussions it will become increasingly evident that all of the chants in the Tu B repertory betray their late medieval origin in many characteristic ways. At the same time, respect for the essential stylistic traits associated with a given category of chant and efforts to conform to those traits are equally in evidence.

The influence of tradition in the settings of the antiphons is particularly obvious in the melodic contours of their opening phrases and in the relationship between those phrases and the psalmtone terminations. Medieval tonaries, as well as modern ones compiled from specific manuscripts, make it clear that each termination was associated with one or more of the characteristic melodic formulas with which the antiphons begin [1]. A detailed study of this association in the forty-four Tu B antiphons should be both interesting and instructive, but we must here be content with a mere indication of what such a study might reveal. The three antiphons for Nocturn 1 in the Hylarion Office provide a convenient example, since they are all in Mode 1 with three different terminations: 1.f, 1.g, and 1.a. In Table 5 the opening phrase of each of these antiphons is compared with an antiphon of the traditional repertory that is assigned to the same ending in the Lucca manuscript. For the sake of clarity, the melodies are indicated by capital letters above the texts. Letters joined by hyphens are sung to one syllable. Where the traditional antiphon as found in LUC has been assigned to a "*thème mélodique*" by Gevaert, his basic form of that theme has also been included in Table 5 [2].

[1] For a brief survey of this subject see W. Apel, *Gregorian Chant* (Bloomington, 1958), pp. 394 ff.

[2] F. A. Gevaert, *La Mélopée antique dans le chant de l'église latine* (Gand, 1895), pp. 225 ff.

Table 5

Thematic Relationships between Antiphons in Tu B and LUC

Termination 1.f

LUC No. 126	D D-C F G F-G-A A A G E-F G F-E D D
	Na- ti-vi-tas tu- a De-i ge- ni-trix vir- go
Tu B, f. 4	C-D F-G-A G-E F-G F-E D C-D D
	De spi- nis y- do- la- ti- cis
Gev. Th. 6 (p. 239)	D C F G A G E F D
[Th. 1 (p. 230)	F G A G E F D]

Termination 1.g

LUC No. 157	G C D D - A -B A
	Ca- ni- te tu- ba
Tu B, f. 4	G C D-C D A B A A
	Mis- sus in A- le-xan- dri- am
Gev. Th. 5 (p. 238)	G C D-A C A G E F D

Termination 1.a

LUC No. 263	A A A D F A G G
	Mi- se- re- re me- i De- us
Tu B, f. 4	A-G A-B A-A D F-G A-G D-E D
	Quan- tum e- tas su- sti- nu- it

The correspondence between the opening melodies of the Tu B and LUC antiphons is sufficiently striking to obviate further comment. Some peripheral matters, however, are worthy of remark. The antiphons assigned by Gevaert to Theme 6, as well as those in LUC that are used with the 1.f ending, almost invariably begin with a clivis D-C. Thus, although it could have been a deliberately introduced variant, one is inclined to regard as a scribal error the opening podatus of the Tu B antiphon *De spinis ydolaticis.* As will appear shortly, moreover, an antiphon *ad Magnificat* in the Office of St. Anne does have the correct opening notes for antiphons of this class.

None of Gevaert's *thèmes mélodiques* seems obviously related to the two antiphons in Table 5 that are associated with the 1.a termination. This ending is normally used with antiphons belonging to Gevaert's Theme 2, of which the prototype is the melody of *Facti sumus:* A G A G E F G F-E D D[3]. Thus, *Miserere mei Deus,* although it begins on A, is completely exceptional among the antiphons of its class in LUC. This fact and the strong emphasis on degrees 5, 1, and 3 of the mode suggest that it may have been a later addition to the antiphon repertory. In any case, the formula A A A D F A of *Miserere mei Deus* clearly underlies the more elaborate melody of the Tu B antiphon. The ornamentation of this basic formula in *Quantum etas sustinuit,* in fact, exemplifies the generally more complex style of the antiphons in the Office of St. Hylarion. As a rule, the antiphons for St. Anne are somewhat simpler in style, and the traditional opening formulas are even more conspicuous. The above-mentioned Magnificat antiphon *Ad felicis Anne festum* provides a convenient example. It is presented here with *Tradent enim vos,* another antiphon *ad Magnificat,* and may be compared with the antiphons in Table 5 that also are associated with the 1.f termination[4].

LU, p. 1112	D	D-C	F	G-A	A-G-G	F	G	G-A	F-E	D
	Tra-	*dent*	*e-*	*nim*	*vos*	*in*	*con-*	*ci-*	*li-*	*is*
Tu B f. 14v	D	D-C		F-G-A	G	F	G		F-E	D
	Ad	*fe-*		*li-*	*cis*	*An-*	*ne*		*fe-*	*stum*

As this example suggests, the greater simplicity of melodic style in the antiphons for St. Anne results from a consistent adherence to a more nearly syllabic setting in contrast to a predominance of two- and three-note ligatures in the antiphons for St. Hylarion. This contrast is clearly evident in Table 6, where the three antiphons for Nocturn 1 from each Office are compared with regard to the number of notes for each syllable. If the figures in this table are reduced to percentages, we find in the Hylarion antiphons 41% of the syllables set to single notes, 50% set to two-note ligatures, and 9% set to ligatures of three or more notes. In the antiphons for St. Anne, on the other hand, 69% of the syllables are set to single notes, 31% to two-note ligatures, and none at all to ligatures of more than two

3 *Ibid.*, p. 233. The melody given here is the version from LUC, *PM* IX, No. 252.

4 *Tradent enim* is listed by Gevaert under Theme 6 (p. 240), appears in LUC under the 1.f ending (No. 136), and is cited by Ugolino among the antiphons that call for this same ending (*Declaratio* I, 105).

notes. These results are representative of all the antiphons in both Offices, although there is a somewhat greater diversity of style than is suggested by Table 6. As is generally true in the traditional chant repertory, the antiphons *ad Magnificat* are among the most elaborate. *Missus in Alexandrinam*, cited in Table 6, is unusually syllabic for a St. Hylarion antiphon, while some for St. Anne are even more syllabic. *Hic ager quem de supernis* (f. 16), for example, has twenty-six syllables set to single notes and only four to two-note ligatures. By way of contrast, however, *Ad legis metas*, the first antiphon for Lauds in the St. Anne Office (f. 18), has only eleven syllables set to single notes, twelve to two, and no less than eight to groups of from three to seven notes. The first antiphon for Lauds in the Hylarion Office is also more elaborate in style than any of the three in Nocturn 1.

Table 6

Differences between antiphons for St. Hylarion and antiphons for St. Anne with respect to number of notes per text syllable

Antiphon	Number of Notes per Syllable 1	2	3	4	5	Total Number of Notes	Total Number of Syllables
	Antiphons for St. Hylarion (f. 4)						
De spinis ydolaticis (8 8 8 8)	10	18	2	1	1	61	32
Missus in Alexandrinam (8 8 8 7)	17	13	1	—	—	46	31
Quantum etas sustinuit (8 8 8 7)	12	16	1	1	1	56	31
Total	39	47	4	2	2	163	94
	Antiphons for St. Anne (f. 15)						
Sol eternus Annam Christus (8 7 8 7)	21	9	—	—	—	39	30
De stirpe patriarchali (8 7 8 7)	18	12	—	—	—	42	30
Ex hac olla spei vite (8 7 8 7)	23	7	—	—	—	37	30
Total	62	28	—	—	—	118	90

Despite this diversity of style, indeed partly because of it, Willi Apel's description of Office antiphons in the standard chant repertory can be applied without alteration to the antiphons of the Offices in Tu B [5]. Just as the Cypriot composers based their opening phrases on traditional melodic formulas, so did they make an obvious effort to maintain an appropriate musical style, at least with regard to characteristic relationships between number of notes and number of syllables. In other respects, however, the antiphon melodies of both Tu B Offices diverge considerably from the distinctive traits of the earlier Gregorian repertory. Poetic texts with a minimum of four lines naturally result in melodies of greater length and more regular phrase structure than are normally to be found among the older antiphons. A wider range, more frequent and wider skips, and a clearly defined tonal organization further distinguish the melodies of Tu B from "*la mélopée antique*". Almost without exception each antiphon in Tu B exploits the full range of its mode, spanning an octave or more often a ninth in the process. Leaps of an octave are rare, although they do occur as "dead" intervals between phrases [6]. Thirds, fourths, and fifths as melodic intervals, on the other hand, are very common, and frequently strengthen the feeling of tonal organization by stressing degrees 1, 3, 5, and 8 of the mode. In addition, the great majority of phrases end on one of these tonality-defining degrees, with the close of the first phrase falling most frequently on the final of the mode [7]. Of the ten antiphons in Mode 1, for example, no fewer than seven end their first phrases on D, while one ends on F, one on A, and one with a clivis D-C. In the total of forty-four antiphons, the first phrase ends on the final in twenty-four (and on the octave above in one), on the fifth degree in nine, and on the third degree in three. Curiously, none of these three occurs in a plagal mode, but each authentic mode except 7 is represented by one example of a first phrase ending on the third degree [8]. Only in Modes 3 and 4 do we find three examples of

[5] W. Apel, *Gregorian Chant*, pp. 392 f.

[6] E.g., in *Fulget sydus*, f. 1, and *Sex unciarum*, f. 1v.

[7] In copying the chants the scribe made no effort to distinguish the phrase endings, and they are not particularly evident from an examination of the music alone. For the purposes of this discussion it is assumed that the end of a phrase coincides with the end of a poetic line.

[8] *Sol eternus Annam Christus* (f. 15) in Mode 1: *Semel in anno abscidit* (f. 6v) in Mode 3; *Scandit sanctus attacoli* (f. 12v), in Mode 5.

first phrases ending on the fourth degree, with none at all ending on the fifth. This emphasis on A, and in other cases on C in Mode 3, is obviously related to the structure of the psalm tones for the *deuterus* tonality. The growing feeling for tonal organization around degrees 1, 3, and 5 of the mode must surely account in great part for the practical disappearance of the Phrygian modes from medieval polyphony. Only in the later 15th century, when they could be supported at the fifth below in an overall tonality of A, did Phrygian tenors return to favor. In any case, the Tu B antiphons in all the other modes reveal an almost modern concept of tonal organization that is, in fact, characteristic of the entire repertory. Indeed, in what follows it will be seen that the traits identifying the antiphons as products of late medieval times reappear in every category of chant represented in Tu B.

GREAT RESPONSORIES

It should occasion no surprise that the great responsories in the Tu B repertory were not even mentioned in the discussion of liturgical recitative. Long before the Offices of St. Hylarion and St. Anne were written the responsorial tones of the verses had been generally, if not invariably, abandoned in favor of freely composed melodies. This is true, for example, of the responsories in the 13th-century Office of Corpus Christi, which are described by Willi Apel [1]. It is equally true of the responsories in Tu B, none of which uses the traditional formula for its verse. Melodies composed *ad hoc*, however, do not preclude occasional reminiscences of the responsorial tones. A melody may begin with the characteristic intervals of the intonation, have brief passages on the reciting note, or close with an approach to the final that resembles the termination of the tone. In the two responsories in Mode 2, for example, both verses begin with a progression drawn from the intonation (C D F G F) and lay brief stress on the reciting note before proceeding in a freer manner [2]. Both halves of the verse in *Felix Anna* (f. 17) begin with the second intonation of Tone 5 and strongly emphasize the reciting note (c′). It should be remarked, however, that the melody of the respond proper lays almost equal stress on the fifth

[1] Apel, *Gregorian Chant*, p. 240.

[2] *Decennis adhuc amenis* (f. 4–4v) and *Celebremus hodiernam* (f. 15v). Comparisons are with the responsorial tones as given by P. Wagner, *Einführung* III, 190 ff.

degree of the mode. The verse melodies of the two responsories in Mode 8 perhaps suggest the responsorial tone most obviously [3]. Near the beginning of the two halves in both verses the normal reciting notes are stressed, *c′* in the first half and *g* in the second. Both melodies near the close have the progression B C A B G A and the final A-G clivis that are found in the middle cadence of the responsorial tone. It is noteworthy that, even where such melodic correspondences exist, there is never any trace of the "invariable and strictly cursive" structure of the terminations of the responsorial tones [4].

The significance of these various, but only occasional, reminiscences of the responsorial tones should not be overemphasized. One cannot know whether they were consciously introduced or result from the unconscious repetition of certain characteristic traits. They may even be merely the products of a creative mind making free use of melodic formulas and procedures common to plainchant as a whole. Certainly it is safe to say that, in general, the verses in the Tu B responsories, like those in the Office of Corpus Christi, "are sung to entirely free melodies, conspicuously different from the responsorial tones in their wide range and fluctuating design which shows no trace of recitation" [5].

Melodies for the opening section of the responsories, the respond proper, are generally classified among the "free compositions" in plainchant, although "within each mode there exist standard phrases which recur in a number of different melodies" [6]. Even in the standard repertory, however, numerous "original" or free melodies stand in opposition to the "typical" responsories, "which are related to each other through some fixed method of composition, such as adaptation, centonization, or free modification of basic formulae" [7]. To the best of my knowledge, the temporal relationship between "typical" and "original" responsories has not been fully established, nor has the evolutionary development of the responsory repertory been fully traced. It seems safe to assume, however,

3 *Anni moram vigesimam* (f. 6-6v) and *Hic anno a vigesimo* (f. 7).

4 Apel, *Gregorian Chant*, p. 238.

5 *Ibid.*, p. 240.

6 *Ibid.*, p. 331. In the following pages Apel discusses at some length the use of standard phrases in Modes 2 and 8.

7 *Ibid.*, p. 341.

that freely composed responds, like free melodies in the verses, became increasingly more frequent in the later Middle Ages. Certain it is that the respond melodies in Tu B show little or no trace of the standard phrases of typical responsories. They could, of course, have been borrowed from earlier sources, as were the melodies of the Corpus Christi responds [8]. The nature of the Tu B plainchant repertory as a whole and of the respond melodies in particular makes such borrowing improbable, but the task of achieving certainty in this matter must be left to other hands.

An interesting survival of the older tradition of responsorial psalmody is the repetition of the verse melody for the doxology when the latter is present [9]. This practice, which clearly derives from the use of responsorial tones for both verse and doxology, provides valuable insights into medieval methods of melodic construction. In many cases, particularly in the Office of St. Hylarion, the verse and doxology differ decidedly in length. The melody of the verse thus requires considerable reworking to adapt it to the shorter text of the *Gloria Patri*. The guiding principle behind such reworking seems to be the retention of melodic identity at the beginning and the end, with deletions in the middle sufficient to prevent a noticeable increase in melismatic style [10].

A striking feature of the Tu B responsories, in fact, is the uniformity of style that is maintained throughout the various sections, responds, verses, and doxologies, of which they are composed. This uniformity, again a matter of the relationship between number of syllables and number of notes, is documented in Table 7, which also reveals subtle differentiation of the individual responsory sections. Somewhat surprisingly, it is the responds proper that have the highest percentages of syllables set to one or two notes. In the verses and doxologies, of course, the decrease in percentages of such syllables is offset by an increase in the percentages of syllables set to a larger number of notes. This increase is more noticeable

[8] *Ibid.*, pp. 341 f and n. 15.

[9] The doxology follows the Vesper responsories and also, as in present usage, the last responsory in each Nocturn. The Tu B chants follow the normal practice for responsories of using only the first phrase of the doxology: *Gloria Patri et Filio et Spiritui Sancto*.

[10] The same procedure may be observed in the responsories for Corpus Christi, *LU*, pp. 928 and 934.

in the responsories for St. Hylarion, since it is concentrated in the syllables with longer melismas of from six to eleven notes. In the St. Anne responsories, on the other hand, the greatest percentage increases occur in the syllables set to only three notes, with the result that the change of style is much less obvious. The stylistic differentiation of the various responsory sections, indeed, is more apparent in the figures of Table 7 than in the music itself. In a given verse or doxology, the actual number of syllables sung to four or more notes is very small, and exactly comparable passages can be found in any of the responds. In part, at least, the slightly more syllabic style of the latter must result from their longer texts. In the more melismatic passages, however, the responds are indistinguishable from the other sections of the great responsories.

Table 7

Differences between responsories for St. Hylarion and responsories for St. Anne with respect to number of notes per text syllable and percentage of syllables with a given number of notes

Responsories	Number and Percentages of Syllables					
	Number of Notes per Syllable					Total Number of Syllables
	1	2	3	4 to 5	6 to 11	
St. Hylarion *						
4 Responds	60 (30%)	101 (51%)	16 (8%)	18 (9%)	4 (2%)	199
4 Verses	37 (29%)	54 (43%)	12 (9.5%)	12 (9.5%)	11 (9%)	126
2 Doxologies	9 (28%)	11 (34%)	2 (6%)	3 (9%)	7 (22%)	32
Total	106 (30%)	166 (47%)	30 (8%)	33 (9%)	22 (6%)	357
St. Anne *						
	1	2	3	4 to 5	6 to 9	
4 Responds	68 (51%)	54 (41%)	2 (1.5%)	7 (5%)	2 (1.5%)	133
4 Verses	31 (42%)	25 (34%)	11 (15%)	6 (8%)	1 (1%)	74
2 Doxologies	12 (38%)	13 (41%)	3 (9%)	3 (9%)	1 (3%)	32
Total	111 (46%)	92 (38%)	16 (7%)	16 (7%)	4 (2%)	239

* The Vesper responsory and the three from Nocturn 1 in each Office are the 8 chants that are here compared.

Other and more significant conclusions may be drawn from the seemingly dull figures in Table 7. When they are compared with the similar analysis of antiphons in Table 6, these figures at once substantiate the more elaborate and melismatic style of the responsories. In four of these chants from the Hylarion Office, 23% of the syllables are sung to groups of from three to eleven notes. In contrast, the three Hylarion antiphons listed in Table 6 have only 9% of their syllables set to groups of notes ranging in length from three to a maximum of five. From the Office of St. Anne, the three antiphons in Table 6 had no syllables set to more than two notes, while the four responsories have 16% with from three to a maximum of nine notes. It is thus quite evident in both Offices that a more elaborate melodic style than that of the antiphons was deemed necessary and appropriate for the great responsories. Tables 6 and 7 make it clear just how, and to what extent, this greater elaboration was achieved.

The figures of Table 7 are also significant for their confirmation of a state of affairs already observed in the comparison of antiphons shown in Table 6. Within the generically more complex responsory style, it is again the examples from the Office of St. Anne that are simpler than their counterparts in the Office of St. Hylarion. Not only do the St. Anne responsories show a higher percentage of syllables set to single notes, but the correspondingly fewer melismas are both shorter in general and have a smaller maximum length than the melismas in the responsories for St. Hylarion. Whether the two Offices were the work of one, or two, or even more, composers, there can be no question that a more elaborate and somewhat ornate melodic style was deliberately and consistently maintained throughout the Office of the saint whose history was so intimately connected with the island of Cyprus.

The more imposing stature and greater solemnity of the St. Hylarion Office are evident not only in the musical style, but also in the poetic texts, which, if not more elaborate, are consistently longer than those in the Office of St. Anne. Texts of the Hylarion responsories normally consist of six-line responds and four-line verses, with the last two lines of the respond being repeated after the verse. Only two texts depart from this pattern. The Vesper responsory has a seven-line respond with repetition of the last three lines after both verse and doxology. The ninth responsory for Nocturns is expanded by one and two lines in the respond and verse respectively. In this case, however, only the last line of the respond is repeated after verse and doxology. In the Office of St. Anne, responsory texts normally consist of four-line responds and two-line verses, but again with repetition of the last two lines of the respond. Here this basic form is expanded in three of the ten responsories. Texts of the Vesper responsory and the ninth for Nocturns have the six- and four-line pattern standard in the Hylarion responsories, while the seventh for Nocturns has four lines in both respond and verse.

It is noteworthy that longer texts stress the importance of the Vesper responsory and the ninth for Nocturns in both Offices. This provides corroborative evidence for the assumption that the Tu B version presents the St. Anne Office in its original form, while the version from Odense is a later adaptation and rearrangement. It will be remembered that this later version suppresses the Vesper responsory, whose text, however, reappears as the eighth responsory for Nocturns [11]. The longest text is therefore out of place, although the seventh Nocturn responsory in Tu B becomes the ninth in Od and is thus longer than any of the first seven responsories. The Odense version, it is clear, represents an intermediate step in the curious suppression of the two most important responsories in the liturgy. No trace of this disrespect for traditional forms is to be found in either of the Cypriot Offices [12].

As the foregoing discussion of their texts has implied, all of the responsories in both Offices have only one verse, the normal form both then and now. After the complete respond and verse, repetition of the last half or third of the respond is indicated by both textual and musical incipits of the section to be repeated. With two exceptions the doxology, where present, is followed by the same section of the respond that was repeated after the verse. The two basic forms are thus $\underset{ab}{R}\ \underset{c}{V}\ \underset{b}{R'}$ and $\underset{ab}{R}\ \underset{c}{V}\ \underset{b}{R'}\ \underset{c'}{D}\ \underset{b}{R'}$. In the third and sixth Nocturn responsories of the Hylarion Office, the last two lines of the respond are repeated after the verse, but only the

[11] See above Table 1.

[12] Documentation of the importance of the Vesper and "climactic ninth" responsories at a considerably earlier date may be found in H. Husmann, "The Origin and Destination of the *Magnus Liber Organi*", *The Musical Quarterly* XLIX (1963), 311-330. Husmann (p. 312) characterizes the present practice of omitting all responsories except those for Matins as "corrupt".

last line is called for after the doxology. The variant form resulting from these different repetitions may be indicated as follows: $\begin{smallmatrix} R & V & R' & D & R'' \\ abc & d & bc & d' & c \end{smallmatrix}$. None of these forms, of course, is in any way exceptional. Their very normalcy, indeed, is the primary reason for citing them here.

The great responsories of the Tu B Offices, like their counterparts remaining in the present liturgy, are the longest, the most elaborate, and formally the most complex of the Office chants. Apart from occasional reminiscences of the responsorial tones in the verses, the melodies are freely composed throughout. They, like the antiphon melodies, tend to exploit the full range of the mode and even to exceed it on occasion [13]. Equally in evidence here is the concern for tonal organization, with emphasis especially on the first and fifth degrees of the mode. Indeed, the brief description of antiphon style given earlier might be applied almost verbatim to the responsories. Only in being more melismatic do the latter reveal a significant stylistic difference, and even this greater elaboration seems sober and restrained when compared with the florid melismas in some responsories from earlier centuries. A single responsory in Tu B usually has no more than five or six syllables set to more than four notes, and melismas of nine to eleven notes rarely occur more than once or twice. There are none of the extended and "exuberant" melismas, often showing a repeat structure, that introduce "a strikingly extraneous element" into many responsory melodies [14]. Sobriety and restraint, in fact, are among the most striking characteristics, not of the responsories alone, but of the entire repertory of Cypriot plainchant.

HYMNS

The remaining Office chants to be considered are the six hymns, three in each Office, which appear in their normal places at Vespers, Matins, and Lauds. These hymns are particularly interesting because, although their melodies seem to be original, their texts in large part are adapted or

[13] The responsory *Decennis adhuc amenis* (f. 4) has an apparent range from F to *b* in Mode 2. It is probable, however, that the first part of the verse (on the first staff of f. 4v) was copied a third too low. If this be true, the total range would be from G to *b*, which is still exceptional.

[14] Cf., W. Apel, *Gregorian Chant*, pp. 342 ff.

taken over *in toto* from pre-existing sources. They thus provide the only poetic texts in the Tu B Offices that establish a definite link with earlier plainchant repertory in western Europe. The hymns are also the only part of the Cypriot repertory that has been studied to some extent and published in a modern edition [1].

As the process of creating new hymns from old is both interesting in itself and revealing of relationships between Cyprus and the West, it may well be documented in some detail. Only the Vesper hymn for St. Hylarion seems to have a completely original text. At least no model has as yet been found, and references to Cyprus and the life of St. Hylarion make the future discovery of such a model unlikely. Even here, however, the last stanza introduces traditional doxological phrases in combination with a final mention of Hylarion's name [2].

The other two Hylarion hymns, *Ordo sanctorum militum* for Matins and *In vasta solitudine* for Lauds, prove to be derived from a set of three hymns in honor of St. Paul the Hermit: *Antiquum throno positum, In vasta solitudine,* and *Ordo sanctorum militum* [3]. That these three texts form a unit is proved by the abecedarian arrangement of their stanzas and by the appearance of the same final stanza in all three [4]. The last of these hymns was extensively reworked to provide the Matins hymn for St. Hylarion. Two stanzas of the latter, the third and fifth, are completely new, while several stanzas of the original have been omitted. No trace remains of the alphabetical arrangement of the stanzas, but the final stanza of the

1 Bruno Stäblein, *Monumenta Monodica Medii Aevi, Bd. I, Hymnen (I)* (Kassel und Basel: Bärenreiter, 1956). The melodies, with the first stanzas of the texts, appear on pp. 127ff., Nos. 197-202. The complete texts of the Hylarion hymns are printed in the *Anhang*, Nos. 19, 39, and 68. Critical notes for all Tu B hymns are on p. 554, Nos. 33-38. Melodies 197 and 198 are for Vespers and Matins respectively, not for Nocturns and Lauds as stated on pp. 127 and 128.

2 The traditional verse *Trino Deo et simplici*, curiously, also begins the final stanza of the Vesper hymn in the Odense version of the Office of St. Anne (f. 284v).

3 *Analecta Hymnica* XXIII, Nos. 451 and 452, and IV, No. 413.

4 The stanzas of the first hymn begin successively with the letters A - H. The second progresses from I to N (with a repeat of H at the end), and the third goes from O to X (Christus) plus H. Only one source is cited for *Ordo sanctorum* (AH IV, 220): "*Diurn. ms. Paulinorum saec. 15. Cod. Gottwicens. 439*". For the other two, however, several sources are listed of which the earliest is "*Brev. ms. Franciscan. Gallic. saec. 14. Cod. Matriten. Bb 166*". (AH XXIII, 256).

original triad appears here unchanged. To facilitate comparison, the two texts are printed here in opposing columns. For the Hylarion hymn from Tu B, the characteristic medieval spelling of the original has been retained.

Original Version
(AH IV, No. 413)

1. Ordo sanctorum militum
Eremitarum humilis
Paulum collaudat inclitum
Et monachorum jubilis.

2. Pauper, mitis et docilis
Caelebs, pius, obediens,
Modestus, sanctus, humilis,
Justus, verus et sapiens.

3. Quaesivit hunc Antonius
Quem Christus ei praetulit,
Panem coelestem nuntius
Jejuno corvus attulit.

4. Rosa fulgens et inclita
Baptista Christo praevio
Paulus Eliae conscita
Consimilis in invio.

5. Suum praedixit exitum
Propheta pandens abdita
Leo deplorat obitum
Flectens genua subdita.

6. Te transitu mirabilem
Sanctorum in splendoribus
De coelis honorabilem
Translatum coeli civibus.

7. Veste nudata praedicat
Antonius, Hieronymus
Laude multa magnificat,
Te, pater pie, petimus:

8. Christi nos auge [munere],
Auctos fove precatibus
Pacis adstringe foedere,
Redde polorum sedibus.

9. Honor et virtus inclitae [a])
Patri prolique genitae
Sacro spirato flamini
Sit sine meta termini.

Tu B Version
(f. 3v–4)

1. Ordo sanctorum militum
Heremitarum humilis
Ylarionem inclitum
Collaudat turba jubilis.

2. Quesivit hic Anthonium
Quem Christus ei protulit
Cujus sanctum commonium
Ad vitam sibi profuit.

3. Hic sanctus it ad nemora
Non leti metu territus
Nec fugit dira verbera
Sed caritate fervidus.

4. Hanc transitu mirabilem
Sanctorum in splendoribus
De celis honorabilem
Translatum celi civibus.

5. Anthonii cucullula
Hunc ornat atque sacculus
Et monachorum regula
Scribit sanctus Hieronimus.

6. Honor virtutis inclite
Patri prolique genite
Sacro spirato flamini
Sit sine meta termini. Amen.

[a]) AH has *inclito* and *genito*, with a note that the words are *inclyte* and *genite* in the Ms. The latter forms agree with the Tu B version and are adopted in AH, with a return to classical spelling, for the other two hymns in the series.

The hymn for Lauds, *In vasta solitudine*, follows the original much more closely than did *Ordo sanctorum*. Only minor revisions make the hymn fit Hylarion instead of Paul, and the one major change is the abandonment of the common final stanza. Newly composed is perhaps too strong a term to apply to the last stanza of the Tu B version, since its phraseology is again traditional for the doxological character of final hymn stanzas [5].

Original Version
(AH XXIII, No. 452)

1. In vasta solitudine
Ut adipis pinguedine
Afflatus sacro flamine
Christum cernit in lumine.

2. Karica pauca pascitur,
Caro jejuna teritur,
Sed spiritus erigitur
Fraus hostis multa pellitur.

3. Latex arentem reficit
Non vini luxus inficit,
Sophia patris afficit,
Paulum virtute perficit.

4. Membra sacrata mollibus
Spretis palmae rigoribus
Operta charismatibus
Refloret et virtutibus.

5. Novit orare sedulus
Fidelis Dei famulus,
Nos meritis et precibus
Jungat sanctorum civibus.

6. Honor virtutis inclitae [d])
Patri prolique genitae
Sacro spirato flamini
Sit sine meta termini.

Tu B Version
(f. 8v-9)

1. In vasta solitudine
- - - adipe pinguedine [a])
Vixit sacrato flamine
Hilarion cum olere.

2. Carica pauca pascitur
Caro jejuna geritur
Sed spiritus erigitur
Fraus hostis multa pellitur.

3. Latex arentem reficit [b])
Non vini luxus inficit
Sophya patris afficit
Sanctum virtute perficit.

4. Membra sacrata acribus
Vincis herent rigoribus [c])
Operta karismatibus
Contemptis pulvinaribus.

5. Novit orare sedulus
Fidelis Dei famulus
Nos meritis et precibus
Jungat sanctorum civibus.

6. Prestet pater per filium
Prestet per almum spiritum
Cui laus sit et imperium
Nunc et per omne seculum. Amen.

[5] E.g., in AH XXIII, Nos. 356 and 357, "*In reversione s. Johannis ab exilio*, have a common final stanza with the lines *Praesta, pater, per filium* and *Praesta per almum spiritum*.

[a]) Under the music Stäblein (*op. cit.*, p. 128) has *----trix pinguedine.* On p. 639, however, he gives the line as *adipe pinguedine* which is the way I read it (beginning of f. 9). The line is still short a syllable, and *ut* plus a note may have disappeared from the end of the last staff on f. 8v. (The first note of this line in Stäblein's version is not now in the Ms.)

[b]) Stäblein gives *Patex* for *Latex*, perhaps just a typographical error.

[c]) The word *Vincis* is omitted by Stäblein.

[d]) This version of the line is the one used in the final stanza of *Ordo sanctorum.*

The texts of the Hylarion hymns, it is clear, range from apparently complete originality to an almost equally complete dependence on a pre-existing model, with *Ordo sanctorum* representing an intermediate stage of extensive borrowings modified and combined with new material. The parallel with medieval methods of melodic composition, especially in later contributions to the plainchant repertory, is too striking to pass unnoticed, and the relationships between the processes of textual and musical composition are certainly deserving of further investigation. Here, they can only be remarked, with the added comment that the Cypriot composers were not without precedent in adapting old texts to new saints. As will shortly appear, the hymn repertory in Tu B itself, limited as it was, provided such a precedent.

In contrast to the hymns for St. Hylarion, all of those in the Office of St. Anne prove to be traditional texts that enjoyed widespread popularity in western Europe. The Vesper hymn, *Lucis huius festa*, is one of the oldest hymns to St. Anne, the first sources cited by Blume being from the 12th and 13th centuries [6]. Textual variants between the versions in Tu B and *Analecta Hymnica* are minor, and most of them are recorded by Blume from one source or another. O *quam mirifica*, the hymn following the Matins invitatory, is noted as being *Ad nocturnum* by Dreves, who lists one 14th- and two 15th-century sources before a printed version in 1521 [7]. Again the Tu B version presents only minor variants, some of which are found in Dreves' sources. This is the hymn that established a precedent, if such were needed, for the Cypriot composer's adaptation of pre-existing texts to fit St. Hylarion. It is clear from the texts printed below that O *quam mirifica* addressed to St. Anne is a similar adaptation of O *quam glorifica*,

[6] AH LII, No. 101.

[7] AH XIX, No. 87.

a Marian hymn whose text and original melody are both attributed to Hucbald [8]. This was evidently one of the most popular hymns to the Virgin Mary, and Blume notes that it still enjoyed a wide dissemination in the 15th and 16th centuries, especially in breviaries of French dioceses [9]. It would be incredible were the original text unknown in Cyprus, and the parentage of the adaptation cannot have gone unrecognized.

Hymn to B.V.M. (AH LI, No. 126)	Hymn to St. Anne (Tu B, f. 15. Cf. AH XIX, No. 87)
1. O quam glorifica luce coruscas Stirpis Davidicae regia proles, Sublimis residens, virgo Maria, Supra caeliginas aetheris omnes!	1. O quam mirifica luce corruscat Celi juncta choris, Anna beata, Celorumque bonis glorificata Inter celigenas etheris omnes.
2. Tu cum virgineo, mater, honore Angelorum domino pectoris aulam Sacris visceribus casta parasti; Natus hinc Deus est corpore Christus.	2. Eya ex te processit proles regia Stirpis Davitice, virgo Maria, Eterni regis, mater et filia, Quem cuntus venerans orbis adorat.
3. Quem cunctus venerans orbis adorat, Cui nunc rite genu flectitur omne, A quo nos petimus te veniente Abiectis tenebris gaudia lucis.	3. Sicut mater prece redde benigna, Augeat ut nobis prospera cunta, A quo nos petimus te mediante Et nunc et semper gaudia vite.
4. Hoc largire, pater luminis omnis, Natum per proprium flamine sancto, Qui tecum nitida vivit in aethra Regnans ac moderans saecula cuncta.	4. Presta pater fili, spiritus alme Eterne Deus nobis confer et nunc Qui semper nitida vivit in ethera Regens ac moderans aera cunta.

Two aspects of the above texts call for further comment. In the first place it should be noted that the text of O *quam mirifica* as it appears in Tu B varies in an unusually large number of details from the version in *Analecta Hymnica*. Only the first stanza and the first line of the second are set beneath the melody, the rest of the text being written below with no music. This method of writing may have induced exceptional carelessness on the part of the scribe, but the character of at least some of the variants suggests that more probably he was copying from an extremely illegible source. In AH, for example, the second line of the fourth stanza has the much more likely reading *Trine Deus nobis confer et une*. The second aspect of the two texts to be remarked is the considerable freedom

8 Stäblein, *Hymnen*, p. 520, notes to No. 48.

9 AH LI, No. 126 and note on p. 147.

with which the original text is adapted for use in honor of St. Anne. The coincidence of lines and phrases is less frequent than in the adaptations for St. Hylarion, and here phrases are even moved from one stanza to another [10]. Nevertheless, the parallels between the two texts are obvious, and the principle of adaptation is unmistakably exemplified.

The final hymn for St. Anne, *Gaudet chorus fidelium,* is published by Stäblein with the text as printed in *Analecta Hymnica,* in accordance with his announced editorial principles [11]. These may be generally valid, but in the present case they lead to confusion because of the variants in the first stanza (all that is given by Stäblein) and in the first word of the first line.

Stäblein No. 202, p. 130 (AH IV, No. 132)	Tu B f. 18v.
Plaudat chorus fidelium	Gaudet chorus fidelium
Coetus canat credentium	Cetus psallat credentium
Annam beatam feminam	Annam beatam feminam
Annam matronam inclytam.	Annam matronam unicam.

Word substitutions of this kind are by no means the only, or the most important way in which the hymn in Tu B differs from the version printed in *Analecta Hymnica.* In the latter, *Plaudat chorus fidelium* is paired with a second hymn to St. Anne, *Felix Maria filio,* the two being unified by a common final stanza [12]. The Cypriot version introduces another type of textual adaptation not as yet represented by the hymns in Tu B, for it combines stanzas from each member of this pair of hymns. *Gaudet chorus,* in fact, consists of the first three stanzas of *Plaudat chorus,* the first two of *Felix Maria,* and a completely different final stanza. Available materials do not solve the problem of which version is to be regarded as the original. Dreves lists only 15th-century sources for the two hymns in AH, but it is unlikely that *Gaudet chorus* should have originated in Cyprus. Moreover this does not appear to be a characteristic instance of the fairly common division of a longer text into two or even more hymns [13]. It would seem,

[10] Compare Stanza 1 of the Marian hymn with Stanzas 1 and 2 of the hymn to St. Anne.

[11] *Hymnen,* p. xvi.

[12] AH IV, Nos. 132 and 133.

[13] Cf. Stäblein, *Hymnen,* p. xvi.

indeed, to be just the reverse. In addition to the common final stanza, *Gaudet chorus* omits the third stanza of *Felix Maria*. Until future discoveries prove otherwise, we may assume that condensation rather than expansion was the constructive principle here involved.

Although none of the types of textual adaptation just discussed is to be confused with writing new texts to old melodies, one might expect that the extensive borrowing of hymn texts in the Tu B Offices would be paralleled by an equal reliance on pre-existing hymn tunes. Such, however, does not seem to be the case. Stäblein does not mention the derivation of the Hylarion hymn texts, and presumably he is concerned only with the melodies when he says that these hymns are unique and the work of a single composer [14]. He makes a similar remark about the hymns for St. Anne despite their traditional texts, each of which appears in Stäblein's volume at least once with a melody other than the one found in Tu B. There seems no doubt, therefore, that all of the hymn melodies in Tu B were newly composed for the Offices in which they appear, and we need not consider the melodies normally associated with the texts. Instead, we may examine briefly Stäblein's assertion that the hymns for St. Hylarion and St. Anne form two stylistically differentiated groups, each of which was the work of a single composer [15].

At first glance the differences between these two sets of hymns are perhaps less obvious than the similarities. Unlike the antiphons and responsories, the hymns for St. Hylarion are not consistently more neumatic than those for St. Anne. Both sets of melodies are primarily constructed with one or two notes per syllable. Three-note ligatures occur once in H 1, twice in H 2 and A 2, and five times in A 3 [16]. Four-note ligatures are found only

14 *Hymnen*, p. 554, No. 33. "Singulär. Alle drei Hilarionhymnen verraten Herkunft aus einer Hand."

15 *Ibid.*, No. 36. "Auch diese drei von der Hilarionhymnen stilistisch abweichenden Annahymnen stammen von *einem* Komponisten."

16 For convenience here and in the following discussion, the hymns are identified by the initials of the saints and the number of the order of their appearance in the Offices. This is also the order in which they are published in Stäblein, *Hymnen*, Nos. 197-202.

Stäblein notes "Melodie über allen Str." for both sets of hymns, but this is correct only for the Hylarion Office. All three of the hymns for St. Anne have the complete melody only for the first stanza.

in H 2, and then but twice. The number of ligatures thus does not clearly distinguish the two sets of hymns, but a decided difference between them appears when we examine the placement of those ligatures. In the Hylarion hymns the final syllable of a line is never set to more than one note, and the penultimate syllable is also given only one note with two exceptions when it has two. In the hymns for St. Anne, on the other hand, five of the twelve lines end with a ligature on the final syllable, and eight lines have a two-note ligature on the penultimate syllable. This avoidance of ligatures at cadential points in the Hylarion hymns seems to be related to a penchant for repeated notes at the end of a phrase. In seven of the twelve lines in the Hylarion hymns, the last two syllables are sung to the same note repeated. Moreover, in the two exceptional lines with two-note ligatures on the penultimate syllble, the last note of the ligature anticipates the final note of the phrase. The latter pattern also occurs twice in the hymns to St. Anne (in A 3), but there is not one instance of a line ending with single repeated notes.

Analysis of melodic motion reveals a further difference between the two sets of hymns. As might be expected, the greater part of the movement in both is stepwise or by skips of a third. In the hymns for St. Anne, however, and even counting "dead" intervals between phrases, the largest skip is a fourth, of which there are only eight. In contrast, we find in the Hylarion hymns one skip of an octave, nine of a fifth, and fourteen of a fourth. These larger and more frequent skips, since they usually involve degrees 1, 4, 5, and 8 of the mode, account at least in part for the greater clarity of tonal organization in the Hylarion hymn melodies. Only by examination of the complete melodies can the strength of their organization around the final as a tonal center be fully appreciated. However, some idea of that strength may be obtained from Table 8, in which are listed the opening and closing notes of each phrase in the six hymns. Roman numerals indicate the phrases, and Arabic, the degrees of the mode, with degrees below the final being preceded by a minus sign. Where they contribute to tonal definition, or strengthen the cadential feeling, notes following the first or preceding the last have been indicated in parentheses. The sign / between numbers designates a ligature. For A 2 (O *quam mirifica*) the eleven-syllable lines have been divided into two sub-phrases, with the semicolon marking the caesura between the sixth and seventh syllables.

Table 8

Opening and closing notes in each phrase of the Tu B hymns

H 1. (Mode 7)

I.	1	—	1
II.	5	—	(5) 5
III.	3	—	(5) 5
IV.	2/1	—	(1) 1

H 2. (Mode 5)

I.	5 (1)	—	(6/5) 5
II.	8	—	(5) 5
III.	1	—	(1) 1
IV.	8 (5/6)	—	(5) 1

H 3. (Mode 7)

I.	1	—	(1) 1
II.	5	—	(2/3) 3
III.	5 (1)	—	(5) 5
IV.	8	—	(2) 1

A 1. (Mode 6)

I.	1	—	(1) 2
II.	1	—	(1/2) 1
III.	4	—	(1) 2/3
IV.	5	—	(1/2) 1

A 2. (Mode 3)

I.	6	—	5/4; 5/6	—	6/5
II.	7	—	3 ; 3	—	5/6/5
III.	8	—	4 ; 3	—	1/-7
IV.	-7	—	4/3; 2	—	1

A 3. (Mode 1)

I.	1	—	(5/4) 5
II.	5/4	—	(4/5) 5
III.	8	—	1/-7
IV.	-7	—	(-7/1) 1

The analysis of phrase beginnings and endings in Table 8 is based on too few examples to permit generalizations as to early 15th-century principles of tonal organization, but it certainly suggests that those principles are worthy of further investigation. It is difficult indeed to believe that the choice of opening and closing notes in the phrases of the Hylarion hymns was not dictated by a conscious desire to establish and stress the organization of the melodies around a tonal center. In each hymn, moreover, the first phrase clearly establishes the final of the mode.

The hymns for St. Anne, at least those in Modes 6 and 1, reveal an almost equally strong feeling for tonal organization. Since much of the stress on the fifth and first (or eighth) degrees of the mode occurs within the phrases, however, this strength is less obvious in Table 8 than it was in the case of the Hylarion hymns. It has been noted before that the Phrygian modes were somewhat inimical to the normal means of tonal organization, but in the case of O *quam mirifica* (A 2) it almost seems that modal ambiguity was cultivated deliberately. The first phrase suggests, if anything, a final on A, and the second is much more suggestive of Mode 7. Not until the third phrase do we find a descending passage from the eighth to the first degree of Mode 3, the final appearing for the first time on the penultimate syllable of the line. It is left for the last phrase, then, to establish this final as the tonal center on which the melody will close. Whether such initial ambiguity was itself regarded as an identifying characteristic of Mode 3 must remain an open question. More importantly, the foregoing description of A 2 suggests that a study of the structural principles underlying even the simple hymn melodies might well prove fruitful.

Only one hymn, *Lucis huius festa* (A 1), has a repetitive formal structure. Here, the melodies for the last four syllables (out of six) in lines 2 and 4 are identical, creating a pattern for which a b c b′ may be taken as an approximate designation. It should also be noted that the first two phrases have an antecedent and consequent relationship with incomplete and complete cadences. Neither of these characteristics is to be found in any of the other five hymns, which may all be classified as through-composed, or as having an a b c d form. It would be a mistake to dismiss them with no more than this remark, however. Repetitive schemes are merely the most obvious way in which formal coherence may be achieved, and the Cypriot composers, as well as their predecessors, generally relied on subtler means. Phrases contrasting in such things as melodic direction, total range, or general pitch level, are combined in myriad ways that defy classification. Only the thoughtful examination of each hymn can reveal the care and skill that achieved formal balance and cohesion without recourse to thematic relationships or melodic repetitions. The chief reward of such an examination, even beyond the greater admiration for the melodies themselves and the better understanding of their underlying constructive principles, is a heightened respect for their composers. Confined within one of the simplest and shortest musical forms, they yet proved themselves to be sensitive and sophisticated artists.

THE MASS OF ST. HYLARION

A complete Mass is inserted between Lauds and Vespers II in the Office of St. Hylarion, where it is introduced by the rubric *Ad missam sequitur Introitus* (f. 9v). Like both Offices in Tu B, this Mass is not merely a collection of plainchant but includes all of the texts, both with and without music, that constitute the Proper of the feast. Most of these texts are Biblical, of course, and they seem to have been chosen for their applicability either to Hylarion himself or to abbots, the class of saints to which Hylarion belonged.

Of the texts without music, only the Secret and the Postcommunion mention Hylarion by name (f. 12 and 12v). A special prayer was also normally included in a Mass for a particular saint, and in the present case it is repeated from the preceding Hours according to the rubric *Oratio ut supra* on f. 10. The important Biblical texts without music are the Epistle (Heb. 13: 9-16) and the Gospel (Matt. 19: 27-29). Since the latter text is still the Gospel in the Mass for Abbots, we may assume that, in the early 15th century as now, the Office for an Abbot was the same as for a Confessor not a Bishop [1]. This would account for the rubric mentioned earlier that calls for versicles and short responses in the Offices to be taken *de comuni confessorum simplicium* (f. 2v). The Epistle of the Hylarion Mass is not now used either for abbots or for simple confessors, but it seems to follow a traditional procedure of continuing at greater length the chapter of Vespers [2].

CHANTS OF THE PROPER OF THE MASS

Biblical texts are used for all the Proper chants with the exception of the Alleluia verse and, of course, the sequence. Because of its special relationship with the sequence repertory of western Europe, the latter item will be discussed in a separate section. The other chants of the Proper will be considered here in the order of their appearance. Attention is particularly directed to traditional usages of the texts and to the survival of generic characteristics in the melodic settings.

> *Introit:* Ego autem cum michi molesti essent, induebar cilicio. Humiliabam in jejunio animam meam.
>
> *Ps:* Convertisti planctum meum in gaudium michi; concidisti saccum meum et circumdedisti me leticia.

The Introit text, which is Ps. 34:13, occurs twice in the modern chant

1 Cf. LU, p. 1206.

2 Cf. the chapter and the lesson in Mass I of the Common of a Confessor not a Bishop, LU, pp. 1196 and 1201.

repertory, once as a Gradual and once as an Offertory [3]. There are a number of variants between these two texts, but the version in Tu B agrees exactly, as far as it goes, with the Offertory text, which is in the Mass for St. Joseph of Cupertino, Confessor. Both texts in LU include the final phrase of the verse, *et oratio mea in sinu meo convertetur*, which is omitted in Tu B. The Introit verse, or psalm, is Ps. 29:14. This text is not in the *Liber Usualis*, but it is listed by Marbach, in the exact wording of Tu B, as being used for both an Alleluia verse and an antiphon [4].

It has already been noted that the normal Introit tone for Mode 5 is used for the verse and also, of course, for the *Gloria Patri*, although the latter text is indicated only by the letters EVOVAE with no music above them (f. 9v). The music for the Introit itself, on the other hand, would seem to have been newly composed. The relationship between syllables and number of notes is in complete accord with the older Introit repertory, in which, according to Apel, "the great majority of syllables carry a group of notes numbering from two to five". However, there is neither the characteristic use of *strophici* nor the introduction of "a snatch of psalmodic recitative into the melodic motion of the neumes" [5]. The melody does, it is true, strongly emphasize the fifth degree (of Mode 5) in the first phrase, and indeed the prominence of degrees 1, 3, and 5 again provides the clearest indication of modernity. The triadic nature of the phrases outlining the F major chord is particularly striking above the words *cilicio* and *jejunio*. It would probably be wrong to speak of pentatonic influence here, although the seventh degree of the scale appears only three times and the fourth but once. Since the seventh degree (*e′*) invariably follows the eighth each time the melody rises to the octave above the final, it must have been regarded as a normal degree in perfectly good standing. The *b*, however, appears only as a sort of lower auxiliary to c′ (above *cum*), and its avoidance to such an extent can only have been deliberate. As will be seen, this Introit is not alone in thus maintaining a pure Lydian mode in a melody that is, at the same time, completely major in effect.

[3] *LU*, pp. 606 and 1646.

[4] "℣ Allel. in Festo SS. Cordis Jesu. Ant. 8. ad Mat. SS. Sindonis D.N.J.Ch." Carl Marbach, *Carmina Scripturarum* (Hildesheim, 1963), p. 101.

[5] Apel, *Gregorian Chant*, p. 306.

Gradual: Dominus adjutor meus et protector meus et in ipso speravit cor meum et adjutus sum.
℣: Et refloruit caro mea et ex voluntate mea confitebor illi.

These are verses 9 and 10 of Ps. 27 as it appears in LU (p. 1739). The only variants in the Tu B text are the insertion of the second *et* (before *in ipso*) and the substitution of *illi* for *ei* as the final word. As they stand, these verses do not appear in the present chant repertory, but part of the first and all of the second are combined in the Gradual *In Deo speravit* (LU, p. 1025) for the eleventh Sunday after Pentecost [6].

In their musical settings, neither Gradual nor Verse agrees with Apel's description of Graduals in general as "the most fully melismatic chants of the Gregorian repertory" [7]. The Gradual from the Hylarion Mass, in fact, is considerably less melismatic than the Tu B responsories. About 30% of its syllables are set to single notes and 50% to two-note groups. The few remaining syllables are sung to groups of four to a maximum of six notes. This Gradual is equally remote from the Gregorian repertory in its avoidance of the standard phrases characteristic of Graduals as a class [8]. Vague reminiscences of formulas and patterns common to plainchant as a whole are not incompatible with the supposition that the melody was newly composed. About the only bow to tradition than can be detected is the effect of a higher range in the first part of the Verse. Although both Gradual and Verse have the same total range (*c*–*d′*), the former is clearly in Mode 1 ending on D, while the first phrase of the latter ranges from *f* to *d′* with emphasis on *c′* as a sort of reciting tone [9]. The Verse ends on *f*, moreover, so that it seems to begin in Mode 5 and ends in Mode 6. This modal contrast between the Gradual and its Verse brings up a question of performance practice that involves all of the chants sung in immediate succession: Gradual, Alleluia, and Sequence.

6 It is also the Alleluia verse "*in Missa pro infirmis*". According to Marbach (Carmina, p. 98), this text is verse 7. For his discussion of the differing verse divisions in the Psalter and the Vulgate, and the 16th-century numbering of the latter, see pp. 21* ff.

7 Apel, *Gregorian Chant*, p. 344.

8 *Ibid.*, pp. 345 ff.

9 A similar procedure may be observed in the Gradual *Universi qui te exspectant* (*LU*, p. 320).

According to some medieval sources, when the Gradual was repeated after the Verse, "the repetition was done on a higher tone" [10]. I do not know whether this practice has been, or can be, documented in the musical sources, but one would like to know whether mere transposition to a higher pitch level or an actual change of mode is implied. The question certainly deserves further investigation, for it must be related to the unusually wide ranges and differences of pitch level so frequently found in the responsorial chants of the Mass [11]. If modal unity was not a desideratum, repetition of the Gradual "on a higher tone", i.e., mode, would have set a precedent for the otherwise inexplicable tonal structure of certain sequences to be mentioned shortly.

In the case of the St. Hylarion Gradual, repetition of the first section in its original form would restore the modal unity, but such repetition had long since ceased to be customary. Jungmann notes that "repetition of the *responsum* after the verse was still customary in the thirteenth century, and in many places even later. As a rule it was first omitted only in those instances in which another chant, the alleluia or a tract, followed, but in most churches it soon disappeared entirely" [12]. Common liturgical practice in the early 15th century, then, makes it obvious that the Gradual verse in Tu B should be followed immediately by the Alleluia, and indeed this mode of performance is suggested by the way the two chants are written in the manuscript itself (f. 10). It seems evident that the Cypriot composer must have regarded the two chants as a unit, for he returns to Mode 1 in both the Alleluia and its verse to produce the following tonal organization:

Gradual	Verse	Alleluia	Verse
Mode 1	*Tritus*	Mode 1	Mode I.

But the series of continuous chants is not yet completed, for a sequence follows the verse of the Alleluia. By the time of the St. Hylarion Mass, of course, the repetition of the Alleluia *jubilus* after the verse was quite nor-

10 J. A. Jungmann, S.J., *The Mass of the Roman Rite*, trans. F. A. Brunner (New York: Benziger Brothers, 1951), I, 428 and n. 43.

11 Cf. Apel, *Gregorian Chant*, pp. 150 f, for examples of both Graduals and Offertories.

12 Jungmann, *op. cit.*, p. 428. In a note to his sentence Jungmann remarks that every repetition was suppressed in the Dominican *Ordinarium* of 1256.

mally suppressed if a sequence followed [13]. This suppression is explicitly called for in Tu B by the rubric *Sequitur sequentia* at the end of the Alleluia verse on f. 10v. With the sequence thus concluding the series of three chants, one might expect it to accord with the tonal organization of the Gradual and Alleluia as outlined above. Such does not prove to be the case, however, for the Hylarion sequence is in Mode 7, or at least the *tetrardus* tonality, throughout.

The sudden appearance of a foreign mode in the final member of the Gradual-Alleluia-Sequence series raises a number of interesting questions. Was there a traditional and consistently maintained modal relationship among the members of this series or between the Alleluia and Sequence? Why did Adam de St. Victor write sequences only in the *protus* and *tetrardus* tonalities, and what governed his choice? Why do some of Adam's sequences, as well as earlier ones, close their first phrases on *g* and their later ones on *d'* a fifth higher? Could this practice have originated in, or at least been inspired by, repetition of the Gradual after the Verse "on a higher tone"? Having thus returned to the starting point of this digression, we may leave these questions for others to answer. Some of them will be touched on again in considering the Hylarion sequence, but definitive answers must await a full investigation of the principles of modal organization as they applied in the later Middle Ages.

Alleluia

℣: Ave sancte Hylarion

The setting of the Alleluia and its verse departs from the traditional characteristics of its class more widely and more obviously than any other chant in the Mass for St. Hylarion. The first unusual feature to strike the eye is the placement of the word *Alleluia* under the melody. If this placement is to be followed, the melisma or jubilus would be sung to the penultimate rather than the final syllable, which falls on the final clivis of the melody. With considerable time and trouble, the significance of this text placement, and whether it represents an accepted method of performance, might perhaps be determined. Certainly it suggests, at the very least, con-

13 P. Wagner, *Einführung* I, 267 and n. 3.

tinuous rather than responsorial performance of the Alleluia melody [14]. When we examine that melody by itself, however, we find that it seems to fall into three phrases, the first of which could be sung to the Alleluia, with the last two functioning as a normal jubilus. All three of these phrases rise to the top of their range with varying degrees of speed before descending gradually to the final of Mode 1. (The ambitus of the first two is *c–c–'*, of the third, *c–d'*.) There is no trace of the repetitive forms characteristic of older jubilus melodies, but the stepwise descending ligatures, appearing both singly and in sequential patterns, may possibly betray the influence of typical Alleluia style [15]. Finally it may be noted that the length of these three phrases — fifteen, twenty-seven, and seventeen notes respectively — suggests a deliberate effort to achieve symmetry of proportion.

The text of the Alleluia verse, as its first line indicates, is specifically addressed to St. Hylarion and consists of ten, eight-syllable lines. With such an abnormally long text, it is not surprising to find that the melody reverts to what may be called the typical style of the St. Hylarion chants, a majority of the syllables being set to one or two notes with occasional longer groups of from three to six notes. There are no longer melismas in the setting of the text, and the jubilus is not repeated at the close. It is possible, however, to regard the melody for the last line of text, *In seculorum seculis*, as an elaboration and extension of the final phrase of the Alleluia. The melodies of the two parts are interrelated in other subtle ways, of which the most obvious, perhaps, is the recurrence of the stepwise descending ligatures that characterize the Alleluia. On the first syllables of *Ave* and *filiis* (f. 10, last staff), they even repeat, on different degrees of the mode, the sequential pattern from the second phrase of the Alleluia. The passage on *filiis* deserves particular notice because it begins on an E-flat, one of the very few accidentals in the Tu B plainchant repertory.

If the melody of the Alleluia verse exhibits almost none of the characteristics of its class, it does at least serve the artistically appropriate

14 One wonders whether William Byrd's "habit of suffixing the Alleluia to the Gradual verse, and then going on to a 'separate' motet for the Alleluia verse" may not have had precedents in the performance of plainchant that are here reflected not only in the text placement of the Alleluia but also in its relationship to the foregoing Gradual and verse. Cf. James L. Jackman, "Liturgical Aspects of Byrd's *Gradualia*", *The Musical Quarterly* XLIX (1963), 36. (See also pp. 20 and 29.)

15 Cf. Apel, *Gregorian Chant*, pp. 386 ff.

function of softening the contrast between the foregoing melismatic Alleluia and the following, almost completely syllabic Sequence. As has been indicated previously, this chant will be given special consideration apart from the other items in the Proper of the Mass. Its existence is recalled here only as a reminder that it does occur in its correct liturgical position.

Offertory: Illustra faciem tuam super servum tuum, Domine; salvum me fac in misericordia tua; non confundar quoniam invocavi te.

This text from Ps. 30 occurs in the present liturgy as the Communion for Septuagesima Sunday (*LU*, p. 501). Apart from the displacement of a few words, the only variant in the Tu B text is the substitution of *illustra* for *illumina* as the first word. That this variant was not the result of carelessness or ignorance is proved by the fact that it too can be found in the traditional liturgy [16].

The melody in Mode 1 is scarcely distinguishable from the other freely composed chants of the Hylarion Mass and Office. A primarily neumatic text setting provides over half of the syllables with two-note ligatures, while nearly a third have groups of from three to six notes. An exceptional group of ten notes seems to occur on the second syllable of *Domine*, but the text underlaying is not unequivocal and the notes above *Domine* should perhaps be grouped 3, 6, and 6 instead of 3, 10, and 2. Only six syllables are set to single notes — an unusually small number for the Tu B chants — and no more than two occur in succession (on the first two syllables of *misericordia*). This absence of short syllabic passages is perhaps the only resemblance between *Illustra faciem tuam* and the older Offertories, which rarely have as many as four or five single notes in succession and never more than five [17]. There are examples of what Apel calls "seventh-formations", which he finds occurring so frequently in the Offertories "that they become a characteristic trait of the musical style" [18]. Since such formations occur elsewhere in the Tu B plainchants, one cannot be sure that their appearance here results from conscious imitation of Offer-

16 The first phrase, with *illustra* and other variants, is listed by Marbach (*Carmina*, p. 104) as a versicle "*in Precibus ad postulandum serenitatem*". The complete text of the Communion, and Tu B Offertory, is verses 17 and 18 in the Vulgate.

17 Cf. P. Wagner, *Einführung* III, 418, n. 2.

18 Apel, *Gregorian Chant*, p. 256.

tory style. One peculiarity of the Tu B Offertory is the use of a B-flat in a rather strange position. After the seventh-formation *d-c f-g-a a-b b-a* on the words *servum tuum*, a B-flat is followed by the ligatures *c′-b-c′ a-f b-a-b-g*. The presence of the tritone — and there are more in the following phrase — suggests that the validity of the flat extends at least until the end of the staff (f. 12, third from bottom). Such a procedure would indeed be an "exceptional trait" in the Tu B Offertory, but on the whole the melody cannot be said to be strikingly distinguished from the rest of the repertory by any "unusually bold formations" [19].

Communion: Elegi abjectus esse in domo Dei mei, magis quam habitare in tabernaculis peccatorum.

This text is Ps. 83:11, with no variants whatsoever. It occurs in exactly this form as the Gradual verse for "*S. Peregrini Latiosi, Conf. Ord. Servorum B.M.V.*" and with some variants as the third Responsory for "*S. Emigdii, Episc. et Mart.*" [20]

In comparison with the preceding Offertory, the melody of the Communion is somewhat more sober and restrained, both in its intervallic structure and in its use of ligatures. Despite the group of six notes on the first syllable, it generally shows the "simple, neumatic style", which Apel says is characteristic of most Communions [21]. In the shorter Communion — thirty-two syllables against forty-two in the Offertory — eleven syllables are set to single notes and sixteen to two-note ligatures. This leaves three syllables with four, one with five, and one with six notes. In both chants, then, half the syllables are set to two notes, but the ratios of single notes to longer groups are almost exactly reversed. Nearly one third of the syllables in the Communion are set to single notes, and one sixth have more than two. In the Offertory, on the other hand, it is the groups of more than two notes that appear on almost a third of the syllables, while only a seventh have single notes. This stylistic differentiation, unobtrusive as it is, may have resulted from a conscious effort to reproduce the generic characteristics of each chant. More probably, however, it represents an

19 *Ibid.*, pp. 363 ff.
20 Marbach, *Carmina*, p. 176.
21 Apel, *Gregorian Chant*, p. 311.

intuitive understanding and unconscious imitation of those characteristics possible only to one steeped in the plainchant tradition.

In summary it is interesting to observe that all of the Biblical texts in the Proper chants of the Hylarion Mass have also been extracted for use in the traditional liturgy. However, the compiler of the Hylarion Mass seems to have used these texts in new chant categories almost as a matter of principle. Only the Gradual text had been previously used, in part at least, for a Gradual. Whatever the reason for this shifting of texts may have been, it certainly left the composer free to write appropriate new melodies, uninhibited by memories of the traditional settings. As we have seen, he managed to endow each chant with at least some of the essential characteristics of its class, and he accomplished this without exaggeration and even without recourse to the extremes of stylistic differentiation to be found in the traditional repertory.

CHANTS OF THE ORDINARY OF THE MASS

The Kyrie is the only complete chant of the Ordinary that is included in the Mass for St. Hylarion (f. 9v-10). It consists of three sections, A B C, with no indication of the necessary repetitions. Although each of the three melodies differs from the others, they do show motivic relationships, particularly in the use of four-note groups descending stepwise. They all place the strong emphasis on degrees 1, 3, 5, and 8 of the mode that is especially characteristic of Lydian melodies in Tu B, and they all close with leaps from the bottom to the top of the range followed by gradual descents to the final. The subtle ways in which these descents are varied yet all arrive at the same cadential pattern is particularly worthy of observation. This Kyrie is listed by Melnicki as being found only in Tu B, and we may assume that it was composed especially for this Mass [22].

The incipit of this Kyrie, which is in Mode 5, is given in Melnicki's thematic catalogue with a B-flat as a signature, although none appears in the manuscript. The Kyrie from Mass cycle 6, in mode 6, is also provided with an unauthorized B-flat signature in her thematic catalogue [23]. This

[22] M. Melnicki, *Das einstimmige Kyrie des lateinischen Mittelalters* (Erlangen Diss., 1954), Mel. 92.

[23] Mel. 121. Cf. Tu B, f. 25v.

discrepancy prompts a brief digression into the general treatment of the *tritus* tonality in the Tu B plainchants. Not a single B-flat is to be found, either as a signature or an accidental, in any of the nineteen chants in Mode 5 or the sixteen in Mode 6 [24]. In a number of chants the need for a B-flat is avoided in various ways. Some melodies use the note *b* very rarely and only as an auxiliary below *c′*, as was the case mentioned above in the Introit. Others use *b* rather frequently, but almost invariably in stepwise descending passages so that it appears in the guise of an unobtrusive passing tone. Ten times in the Kyrie of the Hylarion Mass the *b* appears in this fashion. Only at the end of the second Kyrie does the eleventh and final *b* form with *f* the outer limits of a melodic contour. There are other chants, however, in which numerous tritone relationships and even direct skips from *f* to *b* seem to have been deliberately cultivated. This is particularly true of all five chants in the sixth Mass cycle, and one sympathizes with Melnicki's desire to add a B-flat signature, even though it is without justification in the original source. It is difficult to decide what was and should now be done in the performance of such melodies. In discussing the sequence melodies of Adam de St. Victor, Peter Wagner remarked that "many melodic harshnesses, especially a certain preference for passages containing the *tritone*, lead one to suppose that they originated in France" [25]. Perhaps the similar harshnesses and preference for the tritone, even insistence upon it, in some of the Tu B plainchants may be taken as further evidence of their composers' French origin. On the other hand, the frequent tritones in Mass cycle 6 and elsewhere may have been a deliberate, if inappropriate, expression of deviltry, for which exorcism in performance was expected and required. Since B-flat in the Lydian mode had gained acceptance both in the plainchant repertory and by at least some theorists, there seems to be no reason why it should not have been introduced in performance, and in writing too for that matter. Ugolino of Orvieto, however, says, and quite rightly, that when the fifth from F to C is sung with a B-flat it loses its *tritus* character and takes on that of the *tetrardus* tonality. Moreover he declares that those who do introduce B-flat, even in

[24] These figures include the five chants of a complete Mass cycle in each mode.
[25] Wagner, *Introduction*, p. 240.

the descending form of the mode, understand nothing [26]. Perhaps some such stern eye supervised the compilation of the Tu B plainchants, for their modal purity as written is incontestable. Unfortunately, we shall never know to what extent that purity was maintained in actual performance.

To return to the Ordinary chants of the Hylarion Mass, we find that only the opening phrase to be sung by the celebrant is given for the Gloria. This in itself is strange, for the plainchant repertory of Tu B generally consists of music for the cantors or the choir, and the celebrant's opening phrases for both Gloria and Credo are omitted in the plainchant Mass cycles. A second peculiarity of the Gloria intonation in the Hylarion Mass, the presence of a B-flat in the signature, is explained by the fact that it proves to be the beginning of the Gloria of the present Mass IV transposed up a fourth [27]. From this point on we are left completely in the dark as to what the rest of the Ordinary chants should be. After the Gospel we find only the rubric *Sequitur immediate Credo in unum Deum* (f. 12), while Sanctus and Agnus Dei do not receive even this mention, the manuscript skipping from the Secret directly to the Communion.

If the introductory phrase of the Gloria were intended as a clue to the remaining chants of the Ordinary, we must ask ourselves to what solution it leads. The most obvious would be to use the "authentic Credo" (Credo I) followed by the Sanctus and Agnus Dei of Mass IV. The chants of this Mass were among the earliest to be grouped together and assigned to a special class of feast, and this grouping was maintained more consistently than any other throughout the development of the Mass formularies. According to Dom Catta, all four chants of Mass IV are assembled as a Mass for "*grandes fêtes*" in the great Dominican Gradual of 1254 [28]. Even this may not be the earliest source, for Stäblein finds Mass IV in a Parisian

26 Admittit igitur si per B molle tritus cantaretur formam suam omnino perderet et aliam indueret, scilicet, tetrardi formam, quoad eius partem inferiorem . . . Nihil igitur intellexerunt qui dixerunt tritum in ascensu per b quadrum cantari, et in descensu per B molle pronuntiari. Ugolino of Orvieto, *Declaratio Musicae Disciplinae*, ed. Albert Seay (Rome, 1959), I, 223 and 224.

27 *LU*, p. 26.

28 Dom Dominique Catta, "Aux origines du Kyriale", *Revue gregorienne* 34 (1955), 175-182. Cf. the Table on p. 177.

Missal dating from "after 1218" [29]. He gives the incipits of the four chants as found in this manuscript in *Tafel* 8, and it is interesting to note that, as in Tu B, the Gloria incipit is transposed, although this time up a fifth.

Two objections to the use of Mass IV may be raised, although neither is sufficiently strong to deter one from inserting these chants in the Hylarion Mass should its performance ever be undertaken. In the first place, the four chants of the Ordinary would be the only ones in the Office and Mass for St. Hylarion that were not newly composed for the occasion. The second objection to the use of Mass IV, perhaps even an indication that its use was not intended, is the replacement of its traditional Kyrie. Despite the freedom with which, then as now, the Mass formularies were rearranged and regrouped, it does not seem likely that a traditional grouping of chants associated with the most important feasts would have been chosen only to replace the first member of the group by a completely new chant.

The second objection applies with perhaps even greater force to the use of one of the plainchant Mass cycles in Tu B, each of which is already provided with a Kyrie and is constructed as a modally, if not thematically, unified entity. Modal unity also raises a problem with regard to the intonation for the Gloria of Mass IV. In its untransposed form, this Gloria is in Mode 4 ending on E, but none of the Tu B Mass cycles is in Mode 4, either transposed or untransposed. The intonation as given in Tu B, however, could have been regarded as being in Mode 5 with a B-flat, in which case it would lead nicely into the *Et in terra* of Mass cycle 5 (f. 23v). But beyond the suppression of this cycle's original Kyrie, the incongruity of the B-flat in the intonation casts doubt on this procedure. As we have seen, Mass cycle 5, like all the chants in the Lydian mode totally lacks B-flats, either as a signature or as accidentals.

Most attractive to my mind, although it can never be more than a supposition, is the possibility that one of the polyphonic Gloria-Credo pairs in Tu B would have been performed in the St. Hylarion Mass. If, as was suggested, the transposed intonation of Gloria IV is regarded as being in Mode 5, it provides a perfectly satisfactory introduction to any of the polyphonic Glorias in the Lydian mode with a B-flat in the tenor and

[29] *MGG*, article *Messe*. See section II, beginning in Col. 150, which deals with monophonic settings of the Ordinary.

contra-tenor parts[30]. And if we assume that a polyphonic Gloria was to be performed, we may as well also assume that it would have been one of a pair, with the related polyphonic Credo following in its proper place. Such assumptions would account for the unattached Kyrie of the Hylarion Mass — also in Mode 5 — and certainly it would be difficult to find a more appropriate occasion for the performance of polyphonic Mass movements in Cyprus. This partial solution of the problem still leaves open the question of which Sanctus and Agnus Dei would have been used. Since there are no indications in the manuscript, and since a perhaps excessive number of hypotheses have already been advanced, this question may as well be left forever unanswered.

The Sequence *Exultantes collaudemus*

One of the first extracts from Tu B that appeared in a modern publication was the text of this sequence, which H. M. Bannister printed in 1902 in the fortieth volume of the *Analecta Hymnica* (p. 205). Bannister qualified the poem as a "*kulturhistorischen Kuriosität*" to which he would not willingly deny a place and further commented that "*der Text bleibt vielfach unverständlich*", a remark that applies with equal force to many other texts in Tu B.

Exultantes collaudemus consists of twelve stanzas all constructed after the same pattern: six lines of eight and seven syllables in the arrangement 8 8 7 8 8 7 and with a rhyme scheme of aab ccb. Although the number of syllables remains unchanged in Stanza 10, some variety is introduced by means of internal rhyme and by using the same rhymes in both halves of the stanza. As printed by Bannister, the two halves of this stanza consist of four lines of four syllables plus one of seven, with the rhyme scheme aaaab. Two poetic irregularities occur in stanzas 7b and 12a, where the third lines have only six instead of seven syllables. This lapse must evidently be blamed on the poet, for it was accepted by the composer, who adapted his melody in each case by combining two notes into a ligature (f. 11v and 12). Since this poetic form was highly favored by Adam de St. Victor and subsequent writers, its presence in the St. Hylarion sequence need occasion no surprise. Indeed, at this point in our examination of the Cypriot plain-

30 Nos. 1, 2a, 7a, 8a, and 10.

chant repertory, wonder could be aroused only by radical departures from the traditional procedures of western Europe.

In its formal structure and stylistic traits, the melody of *Exultantes collaudemus* proves to be fully as traditional as its text. Each stanza consists of two structurally identical halves that are sung to the same melody. As a result there are twelve different melodies, each of which is stated twice. (In the manuscript, each half stanza is allotted a complete staff, and each melody therefore appears twice in full.) The twelve melodies follow each other in straightforward succession with no formal variants such as the repetition of melodies in pairs that is found in some sequences of Adam de St. Victor [31]. As will shortly be seen, however, the sequence is much more than twelve unrelated melodies strung together on a thread of text. A simple description of the sequence form as *aa bb cc dd* etc. gives no indication whatsoever that a high degree of creative skill has produced a structural design of great musical interest.

The melodic style, predictably, is almost completely syllabic. Apart from the already mentioned adaptations caused by missing syllables, two-note ligatures occur in only two of the twelve melodies. Melody 2 has one such ligature on the first syllable, while Melody 4 has four, one in each of the first two phrases and two in the third [32]. Syllabic style as an essential characteristic of the sequence is scarcely invalidated by these few exceptions, which are rarer in *Exultantes collaudemus* than in many sequences of Adam de St. Victor.

While the one-to-one relationship between notes and syllables immediately distinguishes the sequence from every other type of plainchant represented in Tu B, there are other and more interesting distinctions. Despite the seeming simplicity of style and form, purely musical organization, both thematic and tonal, establishes an architectonic form unequalled elsewhere in the repertory. Moreover, contemporary with the Hylarion Mass as this form seems to be, it makes use of melodic materials whose ancestry can be traced through several centuries of sequence compo-

[31] E.g., *Laudes crucis* in E. Misset and P. Aubry, *Les Proses d'Adam de Saint-Victor* (Paris, 1900), No. 18, which has the form *aa bb cd cd ee* etc. Essentially the same melody was later used for *Lauda Sion* (*LU*, p. 945), the sequence for the Feast of Corpus Christi established in 1264.

[32] As in the hymns, a phrase is regarded as the setting of a single poetic line.

sition. A complete analysis of these aspects of *Exultantes collaudemus* would result in a digression of unjustifiable length, and we must here be content with justifying briefly the asserted noteworthiness of this sequence [33]. To facilitate matters for anyone desiring to check the statements about to be made, Table 9 contains the complete sequence melody in letter notation.

Table 9

Melody of Exultantes Collaudemus

Mel.	Phrases A	Phrases B	Phrases C
1.	g g a g c′ b a g	c′ d′ e′ d′ a c′ d′ d′	g a b g f g g
2.	c′b a c′ d′ g f g g	c′ d′ e′ d′ c′ f′ d′ d′	c′ a g a f g g
3.	d f g a g f g g	f e d c f g a g	f g a g f g g d f g a*
4.	gd′ e′ d′ f′ g′ f′ g′ g′	d′ c′b a g a f g g	c′ d′ e′ d′ ba c′d′ d′
5.	c′ d′ a g f g a g	c′ d′ f′ e′ c′ d′ e′ d′	g a b g f g g
6.	f g a g d f g g	c′ b a b g f g g	a g a b g f g
7.	a g a b g f g g	d′ f′ g′ e′ d′ c′ d′ d′	g f a b g f g
8.	g b c′ d′ e′ c′ d′ d′	f′ e′ c′ d′ c′ e′ d′ d′	g f g a f g g
9.	d′ e′ d′ c′ f′ e′ c′ d′	g′ d′ e′ c′ g c′ d′ d′	f′ e′ c′ g c′ d′ d′
10.	d′ a g f d e d d	c f e g f g a a	b a g a f g g
11.	g a g c′ d′ c′ d′ d′	f′ c′ d′ b a g a g	b a g a c′ d′ d′
12.	c′ d′ e′ d′ a c′ c′ d′	f′ e′ c′ d′ c′ b a g	f g a g f g g

* Perhaps as a result of a scribal error, the second statement of Mel. 3 has this variant in the third phrase.

One of the most interesting features of this sequence is the manipulation of tonal materials to organize the twelve melodies into four groups of three melodies each. The sequence as a whole is in Mode 7, the normal ambitus of which is strictly adhered to in all but three melodies. These three, which all move only within the plagal range (Mode 8), occupy the strategic

[33] A fuller analysis of the sequence and its melodic ancestry will be found in my article "Exultantes Collaudemus: A Sequence for Saint Hylarion", in *Aspects of Medieval and Renaissance Music* (A Birthday Offering for Gustave Reese), New York, 1966.

positions of Nos. 3, 6, and 10. The apparently irregular placement of the third plagal melody becomes immediately explicable upon examination of the cadence points in individual phrases and melodies. With one exception (Phrase 10B), the thirty-six phrases of the sequence end on *g*, *d′*, or *d*. The distribution of these notes as phrase endings shows careful planning and is worthy of detailed study, but for our present purposes only one aspect of that distribution need be mentioned. There are only three melodies in which all three phrases end on the same note: *g* in Nos. 3 and 6, *d′* in No. 9. Here then are the most obvious means by which division of the sequence into groups of three melodies is accomplished. Groups 1 and 2 close with melodies in the plagal range and phrases ending on the final of the mode. The final melody of Group 3, in contrast, is marked by phrases ending a fifth above the final and by a tessitura near the top of the authentic range. The structural function assigned to this melody obviously precluded using the plagal mode, which now reappears in Melody 10 with great dramatic effect. Thus the plagal mode still fulfills its primary function of setting off the three-melody groups, although its secondary function is now introductory rather than conclusive. Reflecting this change of function is a different treatment of the phrase endings. Instead of ending on the same note, as in Melodies 3 and 6, all three phrases of Melody 10 end on different notes, one being the sole example of a note other than the first or fifth degrees of the mode.

Although further details could be discussed, it is already evident that, without relying on normal methods of melodic repetition, the composer has erected a tonal structure comparable to a traditional A A B A form. Thematic, or at least motivic, repetitions are by no means absent, of course, and provide many subtle interrelationships, even though no two of the twelve melodies are identical. In some instances these relationships seem to be at cross purposes with the quadripartite structure of the sequence as a whole. At other times, however, they reinforce that structure, as is the case with phrase 3C. Anticipated in phrase 3A, and thereby closely associated with the final melody of Group 1, phrase 3C returns intact as phrase 12C to conclude the sequence.

It is scarcely conceivable that a musical form so clear and so obviously organized around G as a tonal center could have been written at any time before the early 15th century. Yet the melodic material of the St. Hylarion sequence was anything but new. Since the poetic form of its text reminded one of Adam de St. Victor, his sequences seem the most likely place in which to seek the melodic ancestry of *Exultantes collaudemus*, and the search is quickly rewarded. None of its twelve melodies, it is true, corresponds exactly with one of Adam's melodies or *timbres* as Aubry calls them [34]. The situation is quite other, however, when we compare the individual phrases (*membres* in Aubry's terminology). No more than one example need be cited, though there are others, to establish beyond the shadow of a doubt the musical parentage of the Hylarion sequence. Its opening phrase, *g g a g c′ b a g*, is also the first phrase of *timbre* 63, the opening melody of no less than four of Adam's sequences. Moreover, this phrase (1A), which never recurs in the Tu B sequence, is likewise used by Adam only as the opening phrase of a sequence. A more obvious acknowledgement of indebtedness at the outset of the Hylarion sequence would be difficult to imagine. Other phrases and an abundance of shorter motives continue the acknowledgement, but independence is maintained, as has been indicated, by avoiding direct quotation of a complete *timbre* from the sequences of Adam de St. Victor. Further discussion of these motivic relationships, of differences in compositional technique, and of the derivative nature even of Adam's melodic material, will be found in my abovementioned article (note 33). Even from the brief description given here, however, *Exultantes collaudemus* clearly suggests that cultivating the neglected field of sequence composition after Adam de St. Victor might well yield a profitable harvest.

THE PLAINCHANT MASS CYCLES

Following the Office of St. Anne, the section of Tu B devoted to plainchant closes with monophonic settings of the Ordinary arranged in six Mass cycles (f. 19v-28). Three of these, Cycles 1, 5, and 6, have the complete form of a polyphonic cycle, including the Credo but omitting the *Ite missa est*. The other three cycles are short masses, consisting only of Kyrie, Sanctus, and Agnus Dei. Perhaps the most important aspect of these cycles is the fact that they are not merely the chance result of an unusual, but by no means unique, disposition of the Ordinary chants.

[34] Cf. the catalogue of *timbres* in Misset & Aubry, *Les proses*, pp. 119 ff.

Instead, their composition as cycles is attested to by the strict modal unity that prevails throughout all five, or three, chants in each group. Although the modes are unequally represented, and some not at all, the cycles are arranged in an ascending modal order, Cycles 1 to 3 all being in Mode 1, Cycle 4 in Mode 2, and Cycles 5 and 6 in Modes 5 and 6 respectively. Curiously, they also reveal an arrangement by increasing order of formal complexity in the Kyries, as will be seen. The coincidence between these two systems of ordering the Mass cycles suggests that they may have been composed by one man, or by a group of composers following a preconcerted plan.

Unlike the usual collections of traditional Ordinary chants, the Cypriot manuscript gives no indication as to the season of the church year or the special class of feast for which any of these cycles was intended. The short Masses correspond with those in the modern editions for feriae and for the Sundays of Advent and Lent [1]. In all of these cases, however, the Credo would also be sung and should have been included, if the practice in the five-part cycles were to be followed here. Perhaps the short Masses in Tu B were intended for such services as those on Rogation days, when both Gloria and Credo are omitted [2]. It seems more probable, however, that they were intended for use with one of the polyphonic Gloria-Credo pairs in the following section of Tu B. It may be objected, and it is true, that modal unity, if it was a desideratum throughout the Ordinary, is not completely provided for by the settings available in Tu B. Three of the Gloria-Credo pairs are in Mode 1, and could be used with the monophonic cycles 2 and 3. However there is no polyphonic pair to correspond with Cycle 4 in Mode 2, and even more importantly, there is no short Mass cycle that could be used with the three Gloria-Credo pairs in Mode 5 or with the pair in Mode 5 transposed down a fourth [3]. But it is, after all, only the unexpected and even unique example of the complete cycles that makes us look for modal unity elsewhere. Since it is otherwise unknown in contemporary practice, there is no reason to believe that it was consistently maintained in Cyprus. In any case, the complete absence of liturgical assignments for settings of

[1] *LU*, Masses XVI and XVII.

[2] Cf. *LU*, p. 841.

[3] The polyphonic Mass movements are to be found in Vol. I of *The Cypriot-French Repertory* . . . (CMM 21).

the Mass Ordinary, both monophonic and polyphonic, is one of the more distressing aspects of the Cypriot collection.

Interesting as it would be, a detailed study of melodic style and formal structure in the Mass cycles cannot be undertaken here. We must be content with a few general remarks about the different classes of chants, followed by a discussion of the historical position and importance of the cycles as a whole.

KYRIE

Perhaps the most interesting aspect of the Kyries has already been mentioned: their arrangement in an increasing order of formal complexity. This may be clearly seen in Table 10, where capital letters under the three subdivisions of the Kyrie indicate sections that are written out in the manuscript. The sign ′ after a letter indicates an extended and sometimes varied repetition. The mode of each cycle has been included in the table to show the correspondence between the two systems of arrangement, and the numbers assigned to these Kyries in Melnicki's thematic catalogue have also been given [4].

Table 10

Kyrie Forms in the Mass Cycles

Cycle	Mode	Kyrie I	Christe	Kyrie II	Melnicki No.
1.	1	A	B	C	181
2.	1	A	B	C	164
3.	1	A	B C	D E D′	165
4.	2	A B	C D	E F E′	196
5.	5	A B	C D	E F E′	8
6.	6	A B A′	C D C′	E F E′	121

All of these Kyries belong to Melnicki's *Formschemata* III and IV, both of which have an overall A B C arrangement [5]. Each group in Class III consists of three identical invocations (*aaa bbb ccc*), and to this class

[4] M. Melnicki, *Das einstimmige Kyrie . . .*, pp. 87 ff.

[5] *Ibid.*, pp. 65 ff. See also W. Apel, *Gregorian Chant*, pp. 405 f. for a discussion of the same four structural types.

the Kyries of cycles 1 and 2 and also of the Hylarion Mass (Mel. No. 92) obviously belong. In Class IV, the middle invocation of each group is a new melody (*axa byb czc*), and Melnicki singles out the Kyrie of Cycle 3 for particular discussion as a transitional stage between the two classes. It is clear from Table 10 that Kyrie I in Cycle 3 is characteristic of Class III, while the Christe and Kyrie II follow the structural principles of Class IV [6]. All this is obvious enough, but when it comes to the Kyries of Cycles 4 and 5, which are identical in form, Melnicki's classifications become inexplicable. The Kyrie of Cycle 5 (No. 8) is correctly listed, without comment, among the Kyries of *Formschema* IV in which the final invocation is subjected to melodic expansion [7]. On the other hand, the Kyrie of Cycle 4 (No. 196) is discussed separately with two other melodies in which the "*Stollenprinzip*" is the form-building factor. Not only does Melnicki give the form of the first two groups as *aab ccd*, but she also says that Kyrie II, in conformity with the lack of melodic relationship between the two bar-forms, consists of three unrelated melodies (*efg*) [8].

An examination of the facsimile (f. 22v-23 and 23v) will show that the Kyries of Cycles 4 and 5 are written in exactly the same way, with absolutely no indication that different manners of performance were intended. Moreover, the form of Kyrie II in Cycle 4 is not *efg* but EFE′ as indicated in Table 10. There are some differences in the writing of ligatures, but E′ is an exact repetition of E that has been extended by the insertion of nine notes in the middle [9]. Since the only forms in Tu B that are completely written out are all ternary, we may take it for granted, it seems to me, that where only two invocations appear, ternary rather than bar-

[6] In her example of this Christe and Kyrie II (op. cit., p. 66), Melnicki gives the erroneous impression that invocations 7 and 9 are identical. Actually, the final Kyrie reduces the five-note ligature of invocation 7 to a single note and adds an extension of twenty notes at the end.

[7] "Melodisches Erweiterung", *ibid.*, p. 66.

[8] Ibid., p. 67 Another Kyrie is cited as having the form *aab ccd ede*. It is possible that No. 196 (Kyrie of Cycle 4) was a typographical error. It appears but once in the discussion of Kyries with bar-form on p. 67, and each of the other two Kyries in this group (Mel. 91 and 208) is found in only one source of German origin. On the other hand, Mel. 196 does not appear where it belongs in the list that included Mel. 8 (p. 66).

[9] E consists of 25 notes. In E′, notes 1-15 are repeated exactly, then 9 notes are inserted, after which E′ ends with notes 14-25 of E. (See f. 23.)

form was intended. The Kyries of Cycles 4, 5, and 6 would thus conform to the Class IV structure found in over a third of the Kyries in the present Vatican Edition [10]. The absence of any indication in Tu B may even be taken as proof that ternary arrangement was so traditional that performance directions were superfluous.

The final Kyrie in Tu B (Cycle 6) is particularly interesting because of the way in which it expands the traditional Class IV structure. Extension of the final invocation was a common and traditional procedure, of course, but applying the procedure in the third and sixth invocations as well makes this Cypriot Kyrie extremely unusual if not unique. Melnicki neither lists it in Class IV nor gives it special mention, and she does not indicate that any other Kyries are similarly expanded. Certainly the procedure is not to be found in any of the Class IV Kyries in use at the present time. It is strange that such a logical development should not have been more widely used, but its appearance in the final Kyrie of the Mass cycles provides further evidence that the increasing formal complexity of the Kyries must have predesigned. The creation of a unique form through the expanded application of traditional procedures must surely have resulted from a deliberate effort to surpass Kyries 4 and 5, in which the normal complexity of Class IV structures had already been achieved.

A final word remains to be said about the Kyries. In her study of many manuscripts resulting in a collection of over 200 Kyrie melodies, Melnicki found the Tu B Kyries in no other source. Therefore it is safe to assume, given their appearance in Mass cycles, that not only the Kyries but also the complete cycles themselves are *unica*. That they were composed at and for the Court of Cyprus early in the 15th century seems equally probable.

GLORIAS AND CREDOS

Since detailed analyses of their stylistic and formal aspects will not be undertaken here, the Glorias and Credos may conveniently be considered together. Appearing in three of the six cycles (Nos. 1, 5, and 6), they give every evidence of being newly composed settings that carefully adhere to the established characteristics of their class. From the formal point of view, they may all be said to agree with Apel's description of some traditional

10 *LU*, Masses III, VI, IX, X, XV, and the first six *ad libitum* Kyries.

Gloria melodies as "essentially free and continuously varying in design" [11]. Their style is almost completely syllabic with an occasional sprinkling of two-note ligatures. Groups of three notes to a syllable are rare, and only two examples of four-note groups can be found. Both of these, curiously, occur on the second syllable of *scripturas* in the Credos of Cycles 1 and 5 (f. 20v and 24v). Each of the six movements ends with a melismatic Amen that provides a welcome relief after the preceding, rather monotonous, syllabic style. Although they are generally more extended than the Amens attached to the Glorias and Credos in the Vatican Edition, their length is not excessive. The Credo of Cycle 6 has the shortest Amen, with thirteen notes, and the Credo of Cycle 5 the longest with thirty. The shortest Gloria Amen consists of fifteen notes and the longest of twenty-seven.

The most surprising aspect of the Glorias and Credos in Tu B is the complete absence of the opening phrases that are sung by the celebrant. Since these movements, in all probability, were newly composed for the cycles in which they appear, one would expect that new and appropriate intonations would also have been written. One would also expect those intonations to have been copied in Tu B, given the nature of its plainchant section as a collection of later additions to the traditional repertory. They are not present, however, and we shall probably never know whether new intonations were composed or old ones adapted for these monophonic Glorias and Credos. The parallel with polyphonic settings of these texts is obvious, and in both cases it is equally difficult to decide which intonations should be used. But perhaps the problem was less important in the 15th century than now. The officiating priests may well have limited themselves to a few traditional formulas, perhaps only one for the Credo, which they used regardless of the musical setting to follow [12]. And if an appropriate intonation were used, the choirmaster certainly could not rely on the celebrant to sing it in tune, at the proper pitch level, or even audibly [13]. Indeed, the complex structures of many polyphonic cycles and

[11] W. Apel, *Gregorian Chant*, p. 410.

[12] A precedent for this procedure exists in the Credos, for the well-known intonation of Credo I in Mode 4 is also used for Credo IV in Mode 1 and is optional for Credos V and VI in Mode 4.

[13] Even some of the "official" modern recordings of Gregorian Chant suggest that the priest may not always have sung the intonations as directed "in a clear voice". (*LU*, p. xv.)

their use of secular materials suggest that concern for any musical relationship with the Gloria and Credo intonations never entered their composers' minds.

SANCTUS

The same structural principles are followed in all six settings of the Sanctus. Although the repetitive nature of the Sanctus text undoubtedly suggested these principles, they are extended to include the repetition of melodic material with different texts. As a result, the musical form of the Sanctus derives in part from textual repetitions and in part from purely musical considerations. In the first section of the text, the threefold repetition of the *Sanctus* is always in ternary form (*aba*) with a free continuation for *Dominus Deus Sabaoth*. The melody for *Pleni sunt celi* is adapted to the *Benedictus qui venit*, and the two *Osannas* are either identical or nearly so. In each of the six Mass cycles, then, the Sanctus has the following five-part form:

A (abac)	B	C	B′	C (or C′)
Sanctus . . .	Pleni sunt . . .	Osanna . . .	Benedictus . . .	Osanna . . .

This uniformity of structure suggests that the Tu B composers were following a well-established tradition, and we do, in fact, find the same formal pattern in many of the Sanctus melodies still in use [14]. As might be expected in these melodies originating at different times and places, the basic pattern is often subjected to greater variation than in the Tu B melodies. Nevertheless, the structural principles remain unchanged, as a few examples will show. The Sanctus of Mass XII (*LU*, p. 50) perhaps comes closest to the pattern established in Tu B. In the opening ternary section (*aba′*), *a′* differs from *a* by the addition of three notes at the beginning; the melodies for *Pleni sunt* and *Benedictus* are almost identical; and the second Hosanna is a literal repeat of the first [15]. A characteristic variation of this formal structure may be seen in Sanctus I, where the *Benedictus* melody varies and extends the first phrase of *Pleni sunt*. The second

[14] In Masses I-V, VII, VIII, X, XII, and XIV-XVIII.

[15] W. Apel (*Gregorian Chant*, p. 417) does not include Sanctus XII in his table of structural types. Sanctus XIII appears twice but neither time in Class 4, where Sanctus XII belongs.

Hosanna then begins with the second phrase of *Pleni sunt* (above *gloria tua*) and continues with a shortened version of Hosanna I. Similar procedures may be observed in Sanctus IV. Here, however, the *Benedictus* melody uses all of *Pleni sunt* plus the first six notes of Hosanna I, after which Hosanna II backtracks to begin with the last five notes of the *Pleni* section before repeating and slightly extending Hosanna I.

Perhaps the greatest variation on the basic pattern is to be found in Sanctus VIII. Apel classifies this Sanctus as throughcomposed but remarks that it is "noteworthy for its repeated use of a short melisma at the end of several phrases, in the manner of a musical rhyme" [16]. Actually, the melisma derives from the tripartite beginning sung to three different melodies (*abc*). At the end of this first section (on *Sabaoth*), *a* and *b* are condensed and fused together, but *c* is repeated complete. Hosanna I consists of *b* and *c* complete, while Hosanna II, after a different beginning, fuses the first notes of *a* with a complete statement of *b* and *c* (on *-na in excelsis*). Moreover, the melodies for *Pleni sunt caeli et terra* and *Benedictus qui venit* are identical, note for note, after which the two sections have different conclusions. It would perhaps be pushing the analysis too far to derive the opening melody of these two sections from the phrase on *Domine Deus*, although that too begins *f a c′* and ends *c′ b* (*flat*) *a*. In any case it is clear that, far from being through-composed, Sanctus VIII has a highly organized form in which the basic pattern A B C B′ C is changed to A B A′ B′ A″. The rondolike effect of this structure is enhanced by transference of the ternary beginning from the first three words to the first section as a whole.

These few examples suggest that a complete study of the Sanctus melodies should be highly rewarding [17]. If those in the Mass cycles of Tu B do not possess all the formal variety and subtlety to be found in earlier melodies, they nevertheless display a structural balance and symmetry that perhaps prefigures the coming Renaissance.

16 *Ibid.*, p. 416.

17 In his discussion of Sanctus form (*Gregorian Chant*, pp. 416 f.), Apel stresses the ternary pattern of *Hosanna-Benedictus-Hosanna*, but he does not mention the parallel structure of *Pleni sunt-Hosanna* followed by *Benedictus-Hosanna*. Since it is actually the musical structure that determines this parallelism, to speak of a "ternary close" is to obscure the essential, and non-ternary, basis of the formal organization.

In its musical structure the Agnus Dei is generally the simplest of the Ordinary chants. The most common form, a ternary ABA, is obviously suggested by the tripartite structure of the text, but ignores the change of the final phrase from *miserere nobis* to *dona nobis pacem*. This form, which is predominant in the chants still in use, is used for the first five Agnus Dei in Tu B. The form of the sixth Agnus Dei, ABB, is so unusual that one is tempted to believe that the scribe copied the wrong melody for the final acclamation [18]. The individual sections of the Agnus Dei in Tu B are essentially through-composed melodies, with only faint suggestions of musical rhyme. In Agnus Dei 6, the last six notes of sections A and B are the same, while in Agnus Dei 5, only the last three notes of each section are the same. There is no instance comparable to several in *LU*, in which the final phrases of all three sections are identical [19].

Stylistically, the Sanctus and Agnus Dei melodies in Tu B are very similar. Except for some rather long melismas on the opening repetitions of *Sanctus*, particularly in Cycles 5 and 6, both chants are written in the predominating style of the plainchant repertory as a whole. The great majority of syllables are set to one or two notes, with an occasional neume of from three to five notes. Equally characteristic is the clarity of tonal organization and the emphasis on degrees 1, 3, 5, and 8 in melodies that cover the total range of the mode. These traits have been repeatedly stressed, and it must be admitted that the degree of sameness pervading the Cypriot repertory contrasts somewhat unfavorably with the richness and variety of traditional plainchant. Within the sober confines of this pervading style, however, and in occasional departures from it, the Cypriot composers achieved a skillful fusion of traditional forms and styles with melodic and tonal procedures characteristic of the early 15th century. The chants in the Offices and Masses from Cyprus, after all, originated several centuries later than even the so-called "decadent days" of plainchant. The proof they offer that the chant tradition was sufficiently viable, even at this late date, to produce worthwhile music of lasting interest is certainly not their least important aspect.

[18] The form ABB does not appear at all in the Agnus Dei in *LU*. Cf. Apel, *Gregorian Chant*, p. 418.

[19] E.g., in Masses II and IV.

A number of factors lead to the conviction that the Mass cycles in Tu B were not mere compilations of pre-existing chants but, rather, were conceived and created as unified musical entities. While not conclusive in itself, the very arrangement in cycles instead of the more common grouping of all the Kyries together, then all the Glorias, etc., is at least a first indication that we are facing a somewhat extraordinary situation. Much more extraordinary, though again not totally without precedent, is the appearance of the Credo in three of the cycles. The fact that no concordances for any of the Ordinary chants have as yet been found suggests that they were newly composed for use in these Mass cycles. And finally, the one factor that obviously makes each cycle a distinct musical entity is the strict adherence to a single mode throughout all five, or three, chants. Modal unity is so strictly maintained, indeed, that there is scarcely any variation even of range among the chants of a given cycle [20].

Musical unity achieved by relating the different chants of a cycle through thematic or motivic repetitions is much less obvious than is unity of mode. Leo Schrade has written that "each of the six cycles unifies all of its movements by identical or similar motifs". He finds a precedent for this procedure in earlier associations of Sanctus and Agnus Dei, but remarks that "union of all movements on the basis of an initial motif, remaining the same or varying slightly, is a different matter" [21]. These assertions, it seems to me, are a bit too strong. Initial motifs, if they exist in cycles 1 and 2, are varied to the point of being unrecognizable. In Cycle 3, however, the three chants do begin with the same succession of at least four notes: *d a g f*. (This pattern does not take into account variants in the form of note repetitions, which are different in each chant.) As an illustration of the somewhat tenuous motivic relationships in the remaining cycles, the

20 The normal range spans the interval of a ninth, the "perfect" form of the mode according to some theorists. However, all the chants in Cycle 4 (Mode 2) have a range of G-*b*. In Cycle 6 the uniformity of range in all chants (*c-d′*) confirms the suspicion aroused by the unusual melodic skips that the phrase *Domine fili unigenite Jesu Christe* (f. 26) was copied a third too low. Cycle 5 shows the greatest variation in range, although it is slight. The basic range of *f-f′* is extended to the note below (*e*) in the Kyrie and to the note above (*g′*) in the Gloria and Credo.

21 L. Schrade, "News on the Chant Cycle of the *Ordinarium Missae*", (abstract) *Journal of the American Musicological Society* VIII (1955), 67.

opening phrases of the chants in Cycle 5 are given in Table 11. Ligatures have been ignored, and the irregular spacing of the continuous melodies is merely intended to bring out the correspondences that do exist.

Table 11

Initial Motives in Mass Cycle 5

Kyrie	c′	b	a	g	f	a	c′					d′	d′	c′					
Et in terra					f	a	c′					d′		c′	b	c′			
Patrem	c′	c′				a	c′					d′		c′			a	g	f
Sanctus					f	a	c′	b	a	g	c′		d′	c′					
Agnus		f	a	g	f	a	c′	b	a		c′		d′	c′					

One cannot know, of course, what the missing intonations of the Gloria and Credo, if they were ever composed, might have provided in the way of motivic relationships. In Cycle 5, however, the initial motive of the Credo as it now stands can be related to the other four movements only by the liveliest imagination. It is difficult to believe that an initial motive deliberately introduced to achieve musical unity would be as deliberately subjected to the more than slight variations in the chants of Cycle 5 [22]. It is equally difficult to determine if other motives in the chants are introduced for the purpose of unifying a large musical structure or merely reappear as basic elements of a rather restricted musical language. The essential unity of each cycle certainly cannot be questioned. Rather than being primarily thematic, however, it seems to me that unity is chiefly effected by a general congruity of melodic style within the framework of a single mode.

Since these unified cycles dating from the first quarter of the 15th century do exist, their historical position with regard to the development of the cyclic Mass cannot be ignored. Until very recently, the cycles of Ordinary chants that appear in the Vatican Edition have been thought to be the invention of their modern editors. As late as 1958 Willi Apel could publish the statement that "the formation of cyclic Mass Ordinaries, each

22 Schrade may have had second thoughts on this subject. At least his article "The Mass of Toulouse", *Revue belge de musicologie* VIII (1954), 85, which contains some of the material of the abstract (note 21), makes no mention of motivic unification in the Tu B cycles.

consisting of a *Kyrie, Gloria, Sanctus,* and *Agnus Dei,* with the *Credos* listed separately, is largely a nineteenth-century process of organization" [23]. In the previously cited articles, which must both date from 1954, Leo Schrade presented the first evidence that arrangement of the Ordinary chants in cycles antedated modern editions by several centuries. In the 14th-century MS 94 in the *Bibliothèque Municipale* of Toulouse, Schrade found the Ordinary chants grouped in "complete cycles", which still means without the Credo, however. This arrangement, according to Schrade, "shatters all the 'standard' views on the subject" and makes the Toulouse manuscript of "extraordinary importance in the history of the *Ordinarium Missae*" [24].

Almost immediately after Schrade's articles appeared, still earlier sources containing the "cyclic" arrangement were revealed, and the importance of the Toulouse manuscript correspondingly diminished, in an article by Dom Dominique Catta [25]. Dom Catta lists all the Mass cycles that appear in ten manuscripts from the 12th to the 16th centuries. These manuscripts, says Catta, "sont loins d'épuiser la liste des Graduels ou Prosaires à Messes composées. *Mais ils ont servi, d'après une note de Dom Mocquereau, aux rédacteurs de la Vaticane pour la composition du Kyriale*" [26]. (Italics added.) Finally, Bruno Stäblein pushed the formation of cycles back still further and showed that *de facto* cycles existed even when their individual chants were not brought together in one place in a manuscript [27]. Stäblein lists no less than six different physical dispositions of the Ordinary chants in which cyclic formations may be discovered. One of the earliest procedures, found in the first manuscripts of the 11th century, intermingled Proper and Ordinary chants in Masses for special feasts. In a second method, the Ordinary chants appeared among tropes of the Proper arranged in liturgical order. Even in the most common arrangement with all the Kyries together, followed by all the Glorias, etc., *de facto* cycles existed as soon as individual chants were assigned to specific feasts. The arrangement in pairs, Kyrie-Gloria and sometimes Sanctus-Agnus Dei, appears in the 12th century, and Stäblein cites manuscripts in

[23] *Gregorian Chant,* p. 405. Later in the same work (p. 419), Apel knowingly departs from this opinion, although he allowed it to stand unchanged.

[24] L. Schrade, "Mass of Toulouse", p. 86.

[25] D. Catta, "Aux origines du Kyriale", *Revue grégorienne* 34 (1955), 175-182.

[26] *Ibid.*, p. 175.

[27] MGG, article *Messe*.

which precise rubrics produce as many as sixteen cycles with an assigned liturgical function. In his Example 3, Stäblein gives the incipits of eight cycles from a French Kyriale in which Cycles 1 and 5 include the Credo [28]. Still another manuscript (Ex. 5) contains two cycles of the Cistercian Order, the first of which also includes the Credo.

This appearance of the Credo in some cycles suggests that another of the "standard" views is perhaps in need of revision. The placement of Credo melodies apart from Ordinary cycles has been generally accounted for on the grounds that the Credo, as the last of the Ordinary chants to be established in the Roman Mass, was never granted full membership in the cycles but was always "treated as a late-comer and outsider" [29]. The strangeness of this argument when the Mass cycles were generally believed to be a 19th-century invention apparently struck no one. And it is still strange, even when, as we now know, the invention took place at least eight centuries earlier. The Credo, after all, was officially established as part of the Mass early in the 11th century, and was certainly in general use throughout the formative period of the plainchant cycles. Purely practical considerations provide a much more likely explanation for the separate placement of the Credo melodies in both medieval and modern chant books. The Credo is a long chant, and the number of Credo settings is almost invariably much smaller than the number of Ordinary cycles. Recopying the Credo for each cycle would have meant a foolish and expensive waste of both manuscript space and copyist's time. Unfortunately, neither medieval scribes nor modern editors gave any thought to what misinterpretations their practicality might lead [30]. In any case, Stäblein's examples of cycles that do include the Credo seem to prove that its more general exclusion resulted from no feeling that it was a late intruder into an already established musical entity.

28 The examples are appended at the end of the article with separate pagination.

29 Apel, *Gregorian Chant*, p. 413.

30 *LU* (1952 edition) has only six Credo melodies but some sixteen cycles with which it would normally be performed. In medieval sources the number of Credo melodies seems generally to have been even more limited. Stäblein discusses the six melodies now in use (MGG, article *Credo*) and comments briefly on the great increase in monophonic Credo settings beginning in the 15th century, apparently influenced by the composition of polyphonic Masses. However, I find no confirmation in Stäblein's article of the assertion that there are about 300 Credo melodies (Apel, *Gregorian Chant*, p. 405).

Whether the traditional Ordinary cycles do in fact constitute musical entities is a question that has received different answers from the modern writers whom we have been citing. Both Stäblein and Dom Catta stress the arbitrary and variable nature of the different cycles, and the lack of musical unity. Modern chant books, it may be recalled, take the same attitude. "This Ordinary is NOT meant to be a matter of hard and fast rule: chants from one Mass may be used together with those from others, the Ferial Masses excepted. In the same way, in order to add greater solemnity, one or more of the following 'chants ad libitum' may be employed" [31]. Stäblein, in fact, entirely rejects the term "cycle" as a designation for the groupings of Ordinary chants and calls them "formulas" instead (*Formulare*). In this way he deliberately emphasizes the fact that, as a rule, musical and motivic relationships seem to have played no role in assembling the formulas. Only here and there in the late Middle Ages were some movements bound together by musical means. According to Stäblein, the earliest known monophonic cycle in which an attempt is made to relate all the movements melodically and tonally is to be found in a Benedictine manuscript that dates from 1452 [32]. And this cycle, be it noted, still does not include the Credo.

In direct opposition to Dom Catta and Stäblein, but before their articles appeared, Schrade had stressed the unity of the plainchant cycles. He began with the statement, harmless enough but not particularly enlightening, that "the order of the Mass in the *Editio Vaticana* occasionally reflects artistic considerations". However, the Masses in which the same melody is used for Kyrie and *Ite missa est* and a few in which two movements show "a melodic association" scarcely justify the conclusion Schrade reaches by the end of the same paragraph. "Thus, a melodic 'motif' becomes an element of fusion among the individual chants of the cycle. The force of the melodic 'motif' gave the cycle an artistic unity. We must lay stress upon the fact that the idea of a musical unity came into being in the province of the plainsong previous to the polyphonic Mass" [33].

It is in the final sentence just quoted that the explanation for Schrade's divergent opinion lies. Not trying to prove anything, Dom Catta and

[31] *LU*, p. 78.

[32] Stäblein, *Messe*, col. 156-157 and Ex. 10.

[33] Schrade, *Mass of Toulouse*, p. 86.

Stäblein were primarily concerned with the origins of plainchant cycles, or formulas, per se. Schrade, on the other hand, was chiefly interested in reversing the "standard" view by proving that polyphonic Masses were composed in imitation of plainchant cycles. For this purpose mere precedence in time was not enough. Musical unity in the plainchant cycles was also essential, if their role of prime mover were to be established incontestably.

Willi Apel seems to agree with Schrade in general, although his assertions are considerably more judicious. Regarding musical unity in the plainchant formulas, Apel merely remarks that in nearly all the present-day Masses the *Ite missa est* is sung to a melody taken from the Kyrie "thus bestowing upon the cycle a noteworthy trait of musical unity". As he rightly says, however, we do not yet know to what extent this is a modern practice based on a few medieval precedents [34]. In summarizing Dom Catta's findings Apel concludes that "the most important result of these discoveries is that they invalidate the theory, generally held until recently, that the idea of a Mass Ordinary cycle had its origin in polyphonic Masses . . . Actually this principle was fully established within the province of monophonic chant at least half a century before it found its first realization in the field of polyphonic music" [35]. No objection whatsoever can be made to the first part of this quotation, but the implications of the last sentence may be open to question. The precedence of the plainchant formulas is indubitable, and, as we have seen, Stäblein proves their existence, not just "half a century", but some three centuries before the first polyphonic Masses. But it must be reiterated that these formulas remain arbitrary and variable compilations of disparate chants. They no more constitute true cycles than the chants of the Proper for a given feast, which were habitually written together in the manuscripts. The fundamental question, and the central point to which this discussion has been leading, still remains unanswered. How, when, and where did the concept of the Mass Ordinary as a completely unified musical entity originate?

[34] Apel, *Gregorian Chant*, pp. 420-421. Apel must have been incompletely informed about the cycles in Tu B (cf. p. 421 and n. 31). It is true that they "show no melodic relationships between the opening and closing melody", but they all close with the Agnus Dei, not the *Ite missa est* whose melodic relationship with the Kyrie Apel is discussing at this point.

[35] *Ibid.*, p. 420.

From a practical point of view the concept itself seems almost nonsensical. We tend to forget, when we examine a Mass in a modern edition or hear it in a concert performance, that it was originally intended for use in a liturgical service, where its sections would be preceded, separated, and completed by other, totally unrelated music. The Kyrie is immediately followed by the Gloria, of course, and no music separates the Sanctus and Agnus Dei, which undoubtedly accounts for the late medieval instances in which these two latter chants are melodically related. But an Introit preceded the Kyrie; a Gradual, an Alleluia or Tract, and often, in medieval times, a long Sequence separated the Gloria from the Credo; an Offertory intervened before the Sanctus; and a Communion followed the Agnus Dei. In such a situation, even a completely unified plainchant cycle might well have passed unperceived. At best it could only have been heard as a sort of unsymmetrical, rondo-like pattern inserted into a larger and musically amorphous structure. When the chants of the Proper were contrasted with a polyphonic Ordinary, however, the sections of the latter naturally stood out in conspicuous relief. It is not surprising, therfore, that complete musical unity is very largely, if not quite exclusively, an attribute of the polyphonic rather than the plainchant Mass.

This attribute, however, is not to be found in the earliest polyphonic Masses. With the exception of Machaut's, the known 14th-century Masses are compilations of disparate movements that may well have been created in imitation of the plainchant formulas. In both cases there is neither modal, nor thematic, nor even stylistic unity. Schrade's attempts to discover "uniformity" in these polyphonic Masses arising from "artistic considerations" in the mind of the compiler I find scarcely more convincing than his discovery of "musical unity" in the plainchant formulas [36]. They are primarily uniform only in their anonymity. Even the Mass of Machaut is unified only by virtue of being for four voices throughout and by being the product of a single, known composer. A degree of unity is also provided, of course, by a general congruity of melodic and harmonic vocabulary. But the Mass is not modally unified: the first three movements end on D with Dorian tenors, while the last three end on F with Lydian or Hypolydian tenors. It is well known too that Machaut did not seek stylistic unity. The

36 Schrade, *The Mass of Toulouse*, pp. 95 ff.

note-against-note style, punctuated by very short, textless interludes, of the Gloria and Credo stands out in sharp contrast to the isorhythmic motet style of the other movements. Finally, the famous "generating cell" that supposedly provided the "basic material" for all of Mauchaut's Mass has now been largely discredited. Bukofzer long ago remarked that this motive, and others of lesser importance, "are not characteristic enough and are not placed conspicuously enough to serve a really unifying function" [37]. Gilbert Reaney included the figure among the characteristic motives of Machaut that were "the most popular ornamentations of the time" [38]. And it has since been shown to be an essential element in the melodic vocabulary of both Johannes Ciconia and the anonymous composers of the Cypriot-French repertory in Tu B [39].

Whatever artistic considerations may have guided the composers or compilers of the 14th-century Masses, it can scarcely be maintained that they achieved a unified structure through purely musical organization. Schrade has decried the view that paired Mass movements, such as Gloria and Credo, or Sanctus and Agnus Dei, preceded the complete cyclic Mass. "Such pairs of selected polyphonic movements are, however, no older than the cyclic Mass; they exist at the side of the cycles" [40]. It is true that paired movements did not precede the cycles — more properly, formulas — that Schrade is talking about. Most of them, in fact, are of even later date. Nevertheless, it is still in the paired Mass movements that we first find consistent efforts to weld separate compositions into a musical whole that is unified by mode, by style, and, to a certain extent, by thematic material. It might be added that, if established procedures with regard to plainchant formulas suggested the composition of polyphonic Masses, the Credo was the least likely text to appear in a paired setting. Given the putative model, indeed, the Credo should never have been included at all in the polyphonic Mass. On the other hand, an *Ite missa est* musically related to the Kyrie should have been one of its essential features.

37 M. Bukofzer, *Studies in Medieval and Renaissance Music* (New York, 1950), p. 218.

38 G. Reaney, "Voices and Instruments in the Music of Guillaume de Machaut", *Revue belge de musicologie* X (1956), 101.

39 Cf. Suzanne Clercx, *Johannes Ciconia* (Bruxelles, 1960), I, 121; and R. Hoppin, "The Cypriot-French Repertory . . ." *Musica Disciplina* XI (1957), 117.

40 Schrade, *Mass of Toulouse*, p. 84.

Be that as it may, no convincing evidence has yet been offered to discredit Bukofzer's position that the complete Mass cycle, with all its movements interrelated by musical means, originated early in the second quarter of the 15th century [41]. And there can be little doubt that such true cycles preceded Stäblein's earliest example of a melodically and tonally unified plainchant cycle, which he found in a manuscript dated 1452. This brings us back, finally, to the historical position of the plainchant cycles in Tu B, and here again exception must be taken to some of Schrade's remarks. Although he recognizes their unusual aspects, he would deny the Cypriot cycles any historical importance. "None of the Torino chants appears in the *Editio Vaticana*; they probably all have a limited local usage . . .; they are most likely to have been composed *ad hoc*." Moreover, the "most unusual inclusion of the Credo is suggestive of an 'influence of extraneous circumstances'." (The final phrase is quoted from Peter Wagner, apparently with derogatory implications.) Finally, "the very fact that the Torino Ms. is a source of polyphonic music, not a chant book, invalidates the application of any inference to the cyclic *Ordinarium Missae* of the chant" [42].

In the first place it may be observed that our concern is not with any inferences applied to the plainchant Mass formulas, but rather with the relationship of the Cypriot cycles to the musically unified cyclic Mass. Secondly, the appearance of these cycles in Tu B enhances rather than diminishes their value, for it establishes both the Offices and Masses as early 15th-century contributions to the plainchant repertory that were deemed worthy of inclusion in a manuscript devoted primarily to contemporary polyphonic forms. Thirdly, the "extraneous circumstances" that caused the Credo to be included, and the *"ad hoc"* composition of the chants for the cycles in which they appear are the very factors that lend these cycles their extraordinary interest. Schrade's rejection of their importance is especially curious, because they are the only cycles thus far known that actually support the argument he was trying to sustain. No longer mere compilations of pre-existing chants, they are real cycles, in which the disparate and disjunct texts of the Mass Ordinary are organized

41 Bukofzer, *Studies*, p. 221.

42 Schrade, *News* (JAMS), p. 67. Cf. also *Mass of Toulouse*, p. 85.

by musical means into a unified whole. And they apparently antedate the complete and musically unified polyphonic cycles.

To over-emphasize the importance of these cycles, however, would be to err in the other direction. There is little likelihood that they served as models for emulation by composers of polyphonic cycles, although Dufay may well have seen then in 1434 at the marriage of Anne de Lusignan to Louis of Savoy. What they do prove, it seems to me, is that the idea of the musically unified cycle was in the air no later than the second decade of the 15th century. That this idea originated in Cyprus is doubtful. Precedents probably existed and may eventually be discovered. Whether the palm for being first will finally go to plainchant or polyphonic cycles we must wait to see. What it is important to note here is that, early in the 15th century at the remote court of Cyprus, composers were already writing true cyclic Masses, perhaps the most astonishing as well as the most characteristic musical contribution of the Renaissance [43].

[43] Much of the material in this final section of the Commentary has already been published in my article "Reflections on the Origin of the Cyclic Mass", in *Liber Amicorum Charles Van den Borren* (Antwerp, 1964), pp. 85-91. It is reproduced here, not only because the presence of the music makes it more meaningful, but also because it forms the logical conclusion to this survey of plainchant composition in Cyprus.

APPENDIX I

COMPLETE CONTENTS OF FOLIOS 1-28 IN TU B

The following outline includes all items in their order of appearance. Texts with music are identified by the complete first line of poetry, preceded by indications of type, mode, and, in the case of antiphons, psalmtone termination. Texts without music are indicated by placement nearer the center of the page. Incipits are given as they appear in the original (with abbreviations resolved), but complete texts are identified by the opening words followed by three periods. All rubrics are preceded by an asterisk. They have generally been translated into English except those identifying the individual Hours. Parentheses enclose text identifications or other indications not in the original. Folio numbers are placed opposite the first item that begins on the page in question.

(OFFICE OF ST. HYLARION)

*In primis vesperis sancti Ylarionis abbatis		1
Ant. 1.D	Fulget sydus ethereum Ps. Dixit dominus (109)	
Ant. 2.D	Gentes laudate dominus Ps. Confitebor (110)	
Ant. 3.g	Hic puer bone indolis Ps. Beatus vir (111)	
Ant. 4.E	Almus pronus obediens Ps. Laudate pueri (112)	1v
Ant. 5.a	Sex unciarum ordei Ps. Laudate dominum (116)	
	Capit: Fratris doctrinis . . . ℟. Deo gratias	
Resp. 6	Letare Ciprus florida	
Hymn 7	Exultans in preconio	2
	*Versicles and responds for both day and night Hours from the Common of simple confessors.	
Ant. 8.G	Sanctus pater Ylarion Magnificat	2v
	Orat: Deus qui animam beati Ylarionis . . .	3
(Matins)		
Invit. 4	Confessorem Cyprium Ps. Venite exultemus (94)	

		Folio
Hymn 5	Ordo sanctorum militum	3v
*In primo nocturno		4
Ant. 1.f	De spinis ydolaticis Ps. Beatus vir (1) *With the rest as in the Common of a confessor not a bishop.	
Ant. 1.g	Missus in Alexandriam EVOVAE	
Ant. 1.a	Quantum etas sustinuit EVOVAE *Nine Lessons are read from the life of St. Hylarion. (From St. Jerome. Cf. *Acta Sanctorum* for October 9, Col. 44a, paragraph 2 and following.)	
	Lesson 1. Ylarion ortus vico thabata . . .	
Resp. 2	Decennis adhuc amenis	
	Lesson 2. Quodque maius est omnibus . . .	4v
Resp. 4	Audiens autem celebrem	
	Lesson 3. Et statim ut eum vidit . . .	
Resp. 5	Statim ut sanctum comperit	5
*In secundo nocturno		
Ant. 2.D	Reversus cum commonacis EVOVAE	
Ant. 4.f	Annorum adhuc quindecim EVOVAE	
Ant. 6.F*	Nudatus induminibus EVOVAE	5v
	Lesson 4. Porro frequentiam eorum . . .	
Resp. 3	Super indutus sacculo	
	Lesson 5. Et parentibus iam defunctis . . .	6
Resp. 7	Carica pauca pascitur	
	Lesson 6. Cunque essent cruenta . . .	
Resp. 8	Anni moram vigesimam	
*In tertio nocturno		6v
Ant. 3.a	Semel in anno abscidit EVOVAE	

		Folio
Ant. 5.c	Nunquam mutavit tunicam EVOVAE	
Ant. 7.c²	Scripturas sanctas coluit EVOVAE	
	Lesson 7. Situs sacco tantum membra . . .	7
Resp. 8	Hic anno a vigesimo	
	Lesson 8. Quid faceret dyabolus . . .	
Resp. 6	Cum caligarent oculi	
	Lesson 9. Iratus itaque . . .	7v
Resp. 1	Cum fatigato corpore	
	*After the last responsory, *Te Deum laudamus* is sung.	
*In laudibus et pro horas diei.		8
Ant. 2.D	Prepotens in miraculis Ps. Dominus regnavit (92)	
Ant. 1.g	Egredere quid dubitas EVOVAE	
Ant. 6.F	O brutus humo propere EVOVAE	8v
Ant. 5.a	Castrum sancti Ylarion EVOVAE	
Ant. 8.G	In castro montis altulo EVOVAE	
	Capit: Fratris doctrinis . . . *ut supra.*	
Hymn 7	In vasta solitudine	
Ant. 1.f²	Benedictus sit dominus Benedictus	9
	Orat: Deus qui animam beati Ylarionis *ut supra*	9v
*Ad missam sequitur Introitus		
Intr. 5	Ego autem cum michi Ps. Convertisti planctum meum	
Kyrie 5	(Complete)	
Gloria ?	(Intonation only)	10
	*Orat: ut supra	
	*Ad Ebreos. Fratris doctrinis varys et peregrinis . . . (Heb. 13:9-16)	
Grad. 1	Dominus adjutor meus V. Et refloruit caro mea	

		Folio
Allel. 1	Alleluya	
	V. Ave sancte Hylarion	
	*Sequitur sequentia	
Seq. 7	Exultantes collaudemus	10v
	*Secundum Mattheum (19.d): In illo tempore . . .	12
	*Credo in unum Deo follows immediately.	
Off. 1	Illustra faciem tuam	
	Secret. Secretorum . . .	
Comm.	Elegi abjectus esse	
	Postcomm: Spiritalis alimonie . . .	12v

*In secundis vesperis

Ant. 7.c	Ylarion de tenebris EVOVAE	
Ant. 8.c	Hic vitam heremeticam EVOVAE	
Ant. 5.a	Scandit sanctus atta coli EVOVAE	
Ant. 6.F	Exultet Cyprus fertilis EVOVAE	
Ant. 3.g[2]	Post labores fructiferos EVOVAE	13
	*Psalms, chapter, hymn, and versicles are said as in first Vespers.	
Ant. 2.D	Cum corpus hoc examine Magnificat	
	Orat: Deus qui animam *ut supra.*	

(OFFICE OF ST. ANNE)

*In festo beate Anne, matris virginis Marie. Ad vesperas.		14
	Capit: Mulierem fortem quis inveniet . . . ℟. Deo gratias.	
Resp. 5	Inter legis sacramenta	
Hymn 6	Lucis huius festa	
	Versicle: Diffusa est gratia.	14v
Ant. 1.f	Ad felicis Anne festum Magnificat	
	Orat: Deus qui beate Anne . . .	

		Folio
(Matins)		
Invit. 4	Adoremus Christum regem	
	Ps. Venite (94)	
Hymn 3	O quam mirifica luce corruscat	15
*In primo nocturno		
Ant. 1.g^2	Sol eternus Annam Christus	
	Ps. Domine dominus noster (8)	
Ant. 3.a	De stirpe patriarchali	
	Ps. Celi enarrant (18)	
Ant. 5.a	Ex hac olla spei vite	
	Ps. Domini est terra (23)	
	Versicle: Specie tua.	
	Lesson 1. Postulastis filie . . .	
Resp. 2	Celebremus hodiernam	15v
	Lesson 2. Ergo mulieres . . .	
Resp. 4	In redemptionis nostre	
	Lesson 3. Verumtamen quem vestre . . .	
Resp. 6	Bethleem natale solum	
*In secundo nocturno		16
Ant. 6.F*	Abrae beati senis	
	Ps. Eructavit (44)	
Ant. 7.c	Hic ager quem de supernis	
	Ps. Deus noster refugium (45)	
Ant. 8.G	Annam juda germinavit	
	Ps. Fundamenta (86)	
Vcle.	Adjuvabit eam Deus	
	Lesson 4. Ergo mulieres . . .	
Resp. 1	Mediante nobis Anna	
	Lesson 5. Igitur in hystoriis . . .	16v
Resp. 3	Sindonem virginitatis	
	Lesson 6. Qua propter ut Deus . . .	
Resp. 7	Genealogie Christi	
*In tertio nocturno		
Ant. 5.a	Hec ad opus matris Christi	
	Ps. Cantate primus (95)	
Ant. 7.a	Linea virginitatis	17
	Ps. Dominus regnavit exsultet terra (96)	

Folio

Ant. 4.E	Dignum genetrici sue EVOVAE	
	*Secundum Mattheum. In illo tempore . . . (Matt. 13.f)	
	Lesson 7. *Omelia sancti Gregorii pape. Celorum que regnum . . .	
Resp. 5	Felix Anna que Samuelem	
	Lesson 8. Non enim congruum fuit . . .	17v
Resp. 6	Omnia prophetas longeva	
	Lesson 9. Legitur in perfecta ystoria . . .	
Resp. 1	Rex dilecte matris Anne	
*In laudibus		18
Ant. 1.D	Ad legis metas fidei Ps. Dominus regnavit (92) *With the rest. (Psalms for Lauds of Feasts?)	
Ant. 2.D	Concives late EVOVAE	
Ant. 3.b	Anna Deo vigilat eo EVOVAE	
Ant. 5.a	Eximia celebris EVOVAE	
Ant. 6.F	Laudem de celis EVOVAE	
	Capit: Mulierem fortem etc. *ut supra*	18v
Hymn 1	Gaudet chorus fidelium	
	Versicle: Elegit eam Dominus	
Ant. 1.a	Hodie splendor eterni Benedictus	
	*Orat: *ut supra*	
*Ad iii.		
	Capit: Mulierem fortem . . . *Responsories are said from the Common of Virgins.	
*Ad vi.		
	Capit: Aperuit mulier fortis . . . ℟. Deo gratias	
*Ad ix.		
	Capit: Accinxit fortitudine . . .	19

Folio

*Ad Vesperas

*Antiphons of Lauds. Psalms from the Common of Virgins.

*Capit: Mulierem fortem

*Resp. Genealogie

*Hymn Lucis huius

Vcle: Diffusa est gratia

Ant. 5.a Anna parens matris
Magnificat

*Orat: *ut supra*

(MASS CYCLES)

Kyrie	19v	Kyrie	22v
Et in terra	19v	Sanctus	23
Patrem	20	Agnus Dei	23
Sanctus	21v		
Agnus Dei	21v	Kyrie	23v
		Et in terra	23v
Kyrie	21v	Patrem	24
Sanctus	22	Sanctus	25v
Agnus Dei	22	Agnus Dei	25v
Kyrie	22	Kyrie	25v
Sanctus	22v	Et in terra	26
Agnus Dei	22v	Patrem	26v
		Sanctus	27v
		Agnus Dei	27v

APPENDIX II

ALPHABETICAL INDEX OF CHANTS

(excluding the Mass Cycles)

Mode [1]	Incipit	Type	Folio
6.F*	Abrae beati senis	Ant.	16
1.f	Ad felicis Anne festum	Ant. ad Mag.	14v
1.D	Ad legis metas	Ant.	18
4	Adoremus Christum regem	Invit.	14v
4.E	Almus pronus obediens	Ant.	1v
3.b	Anna Deo vigilat eo	Ant.	18
8.G	Annam juda germinavit	Ant.	16
5.a	Anna parens matris	Ant. ad Mag.	19
8	Anni moram vigesimam	Resp.	6
4.f	Annorum adhuc quindecim	Ant.	5
4	Audiens autem celebrem	Resp.	4v
1	Ave sancte Hylarion	Allel. Verse	10
1.f2	Benedictus sit dominus	Ant. ad Bened.	9
6	Bethleem natale solum	Resp.	15v
7	Carica pauca pascitur	Resp.	6
5.a	Castrum sancti Ylarion	Ant.	8v
2	Celebremus hodiernam	Resp.	15v
2.D	Concives late	Ant.	18
4	Confessorem Cyprium	Invit.	3
6	Cum caligarent oculi	Resp.	7
2.D	Cum corpus hoc examine	Ant. ad Mag.	13
1	Cum fatigato corpore	Resp.	7v
2	Decennis adhuc amenis	Resp.	4
1.f	De spinis ydolaticis	Ant.	4
3.a	De stirpe patriarchali	Ant.	15

[1] Both mode and psalm-tone terminations are given for antiphons. (See Table 4, pp. 35 ff.)

Mode	Incipit	Type	Folio
4.E	Dignum genetrici sue	Ant.	17
1	Dominus adjutor meus	Grad.	10
5	Ego autem cum michi	Intr.	9v
1.g	Egredere quid dubitas	Ant.	8
6	Elegi abjectus	Comm.	12
5.a	Ex hac olla spei vite	Ant.	15
5.a	Eximia celebris	Ant.	18
7	Exultans in preconio	Hymn	2
7	Exultantes collaudemus	Seq.	10v
6.F	Exultet Cyprus fertilis	Ant.	12v
5	Felix Anna que Samuelem	Resp.	17
1.D	Fulget sydus ethereum	Ant.	1
1	Gaudet chorus fidelium	Hymn	18v
7	Genealogie Christi	Resp.	16v
2.D	Gentes laudate dominus	Ant.	1
5.a	Hec ad opus matris Christi	Ant.	16v
7.c	Hic ager quem de supernis	Ant.	16
8	Hic anno a vigesimo	Resp.	7
3.g	Hic puer bone indolis	Ant.	1
8.c	Hic vitam heremeticam	Ant.	12v
1.a	Hodie splendor eterni	Ant. ad Bened.	18v
1	Illustra faciem tuam	Off.	12
8.G	In castro montis altulo	Ant.	8v
4	In redemptionis nostre	Resp.	15v
5	Inter legis sacramenta	Resp.	14
7	In vasta solitudine	Hymn	8v
6.F	Laudem de celis	Ant.	18
6	Letare Ciprus florida	Resp.	1v
7.a	Linea virginitatis	Ant.	17
6	Lucis huius festa	Hymn	14

Mode	Incipit	Type	Folio
1	Mediante nobis Anna	Resp.	16
1.g	Missus in Alexandriam	Ant.	4
6.F*	Nudatus induminibus	Ant.	5v
5.c	Nunquam mutavit tunicam	Ant.	6v
6.F	O brutus humo propere	Ant.	8v
6	Omnia prophetas longeva	Resp.	17v
3	O quam mirifica	Hymn	15
5	Ordo sanctorum militum	Hymn	3v
3.g2	Post labores fructiferos	Ant.	13
2.D	Prepotens in miraculis	Ant.	8
1.a	Quantum etas sustinuit	Ant.	4
2.D	Reversus cum commonacis	Ant.	5
1	Rex dilecte matris Anne	Resp.	17v
8.G	Sanctus pater Ylarion	Ant. ad Mag.	2v
5.a	Scandit sanctus atta coli	Ant.	12v
7.c2	Scripturas sanctas coluit	Ant.	6v
3.a	Semel in anno abscidit	Ant.	6v
5.a	Sex unciarum ordei	Ant.	1v
3	Sindonem virginitatis	Resp.	16v
1.g2	Sol eternus Annam Christus	Ant.	15
5	Statim ut sanctum comperit	Resp.	5
3	Super indutus sacculo	Resp.	5v
7.c	Ylarion de tenebris	Ant.	12v

FACSIMILES

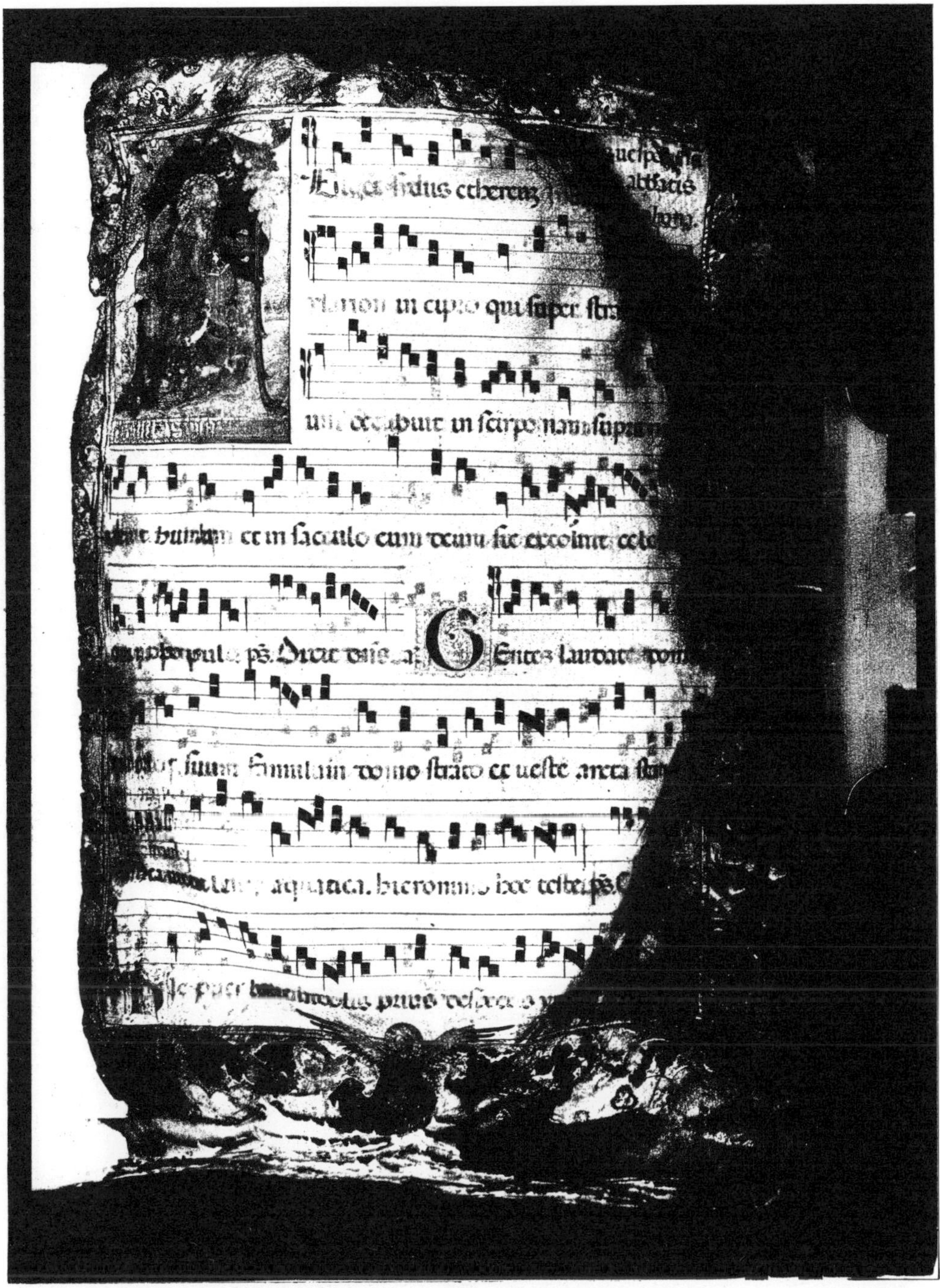

(Folio 1)

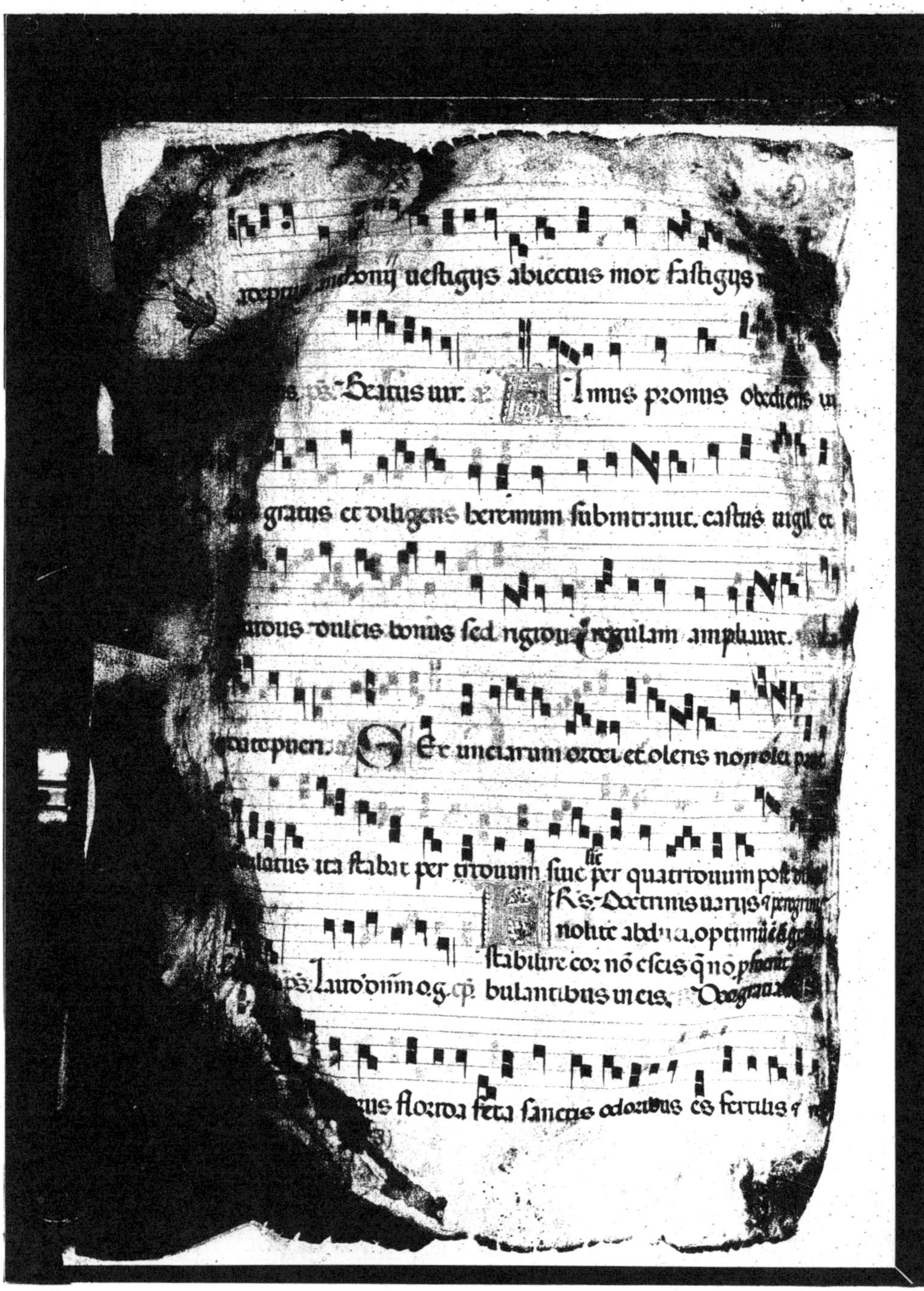

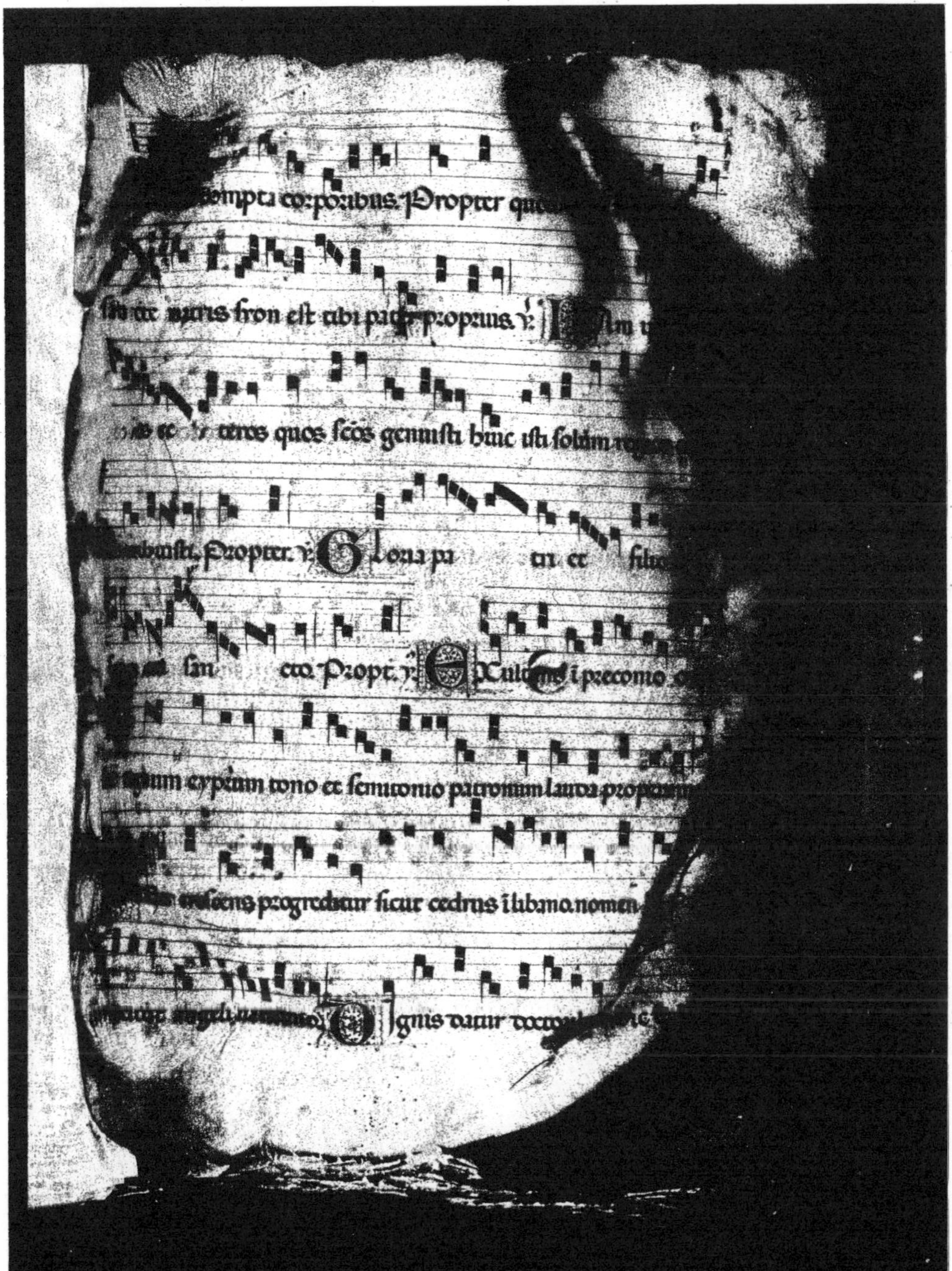

(Folio 2)

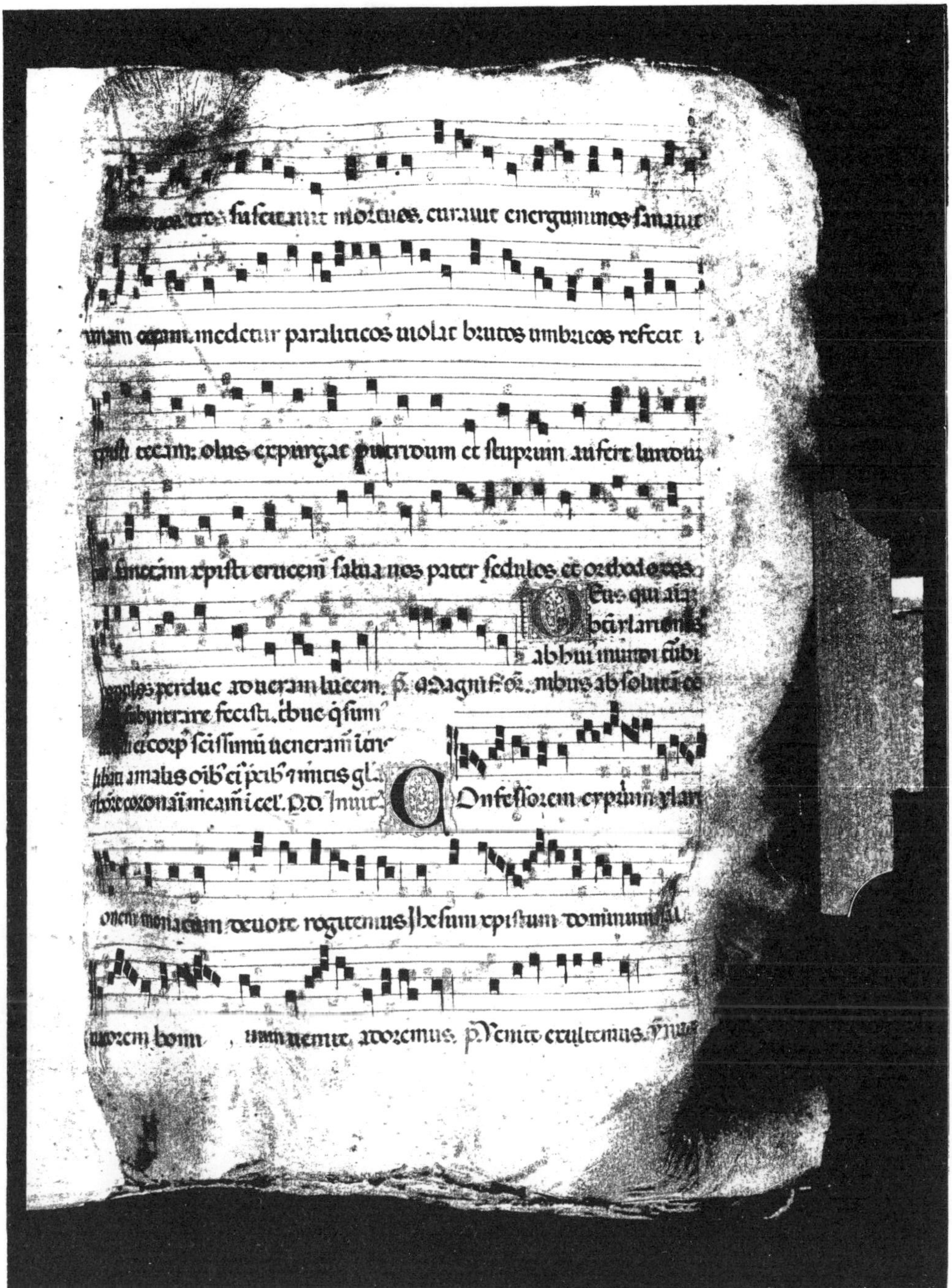

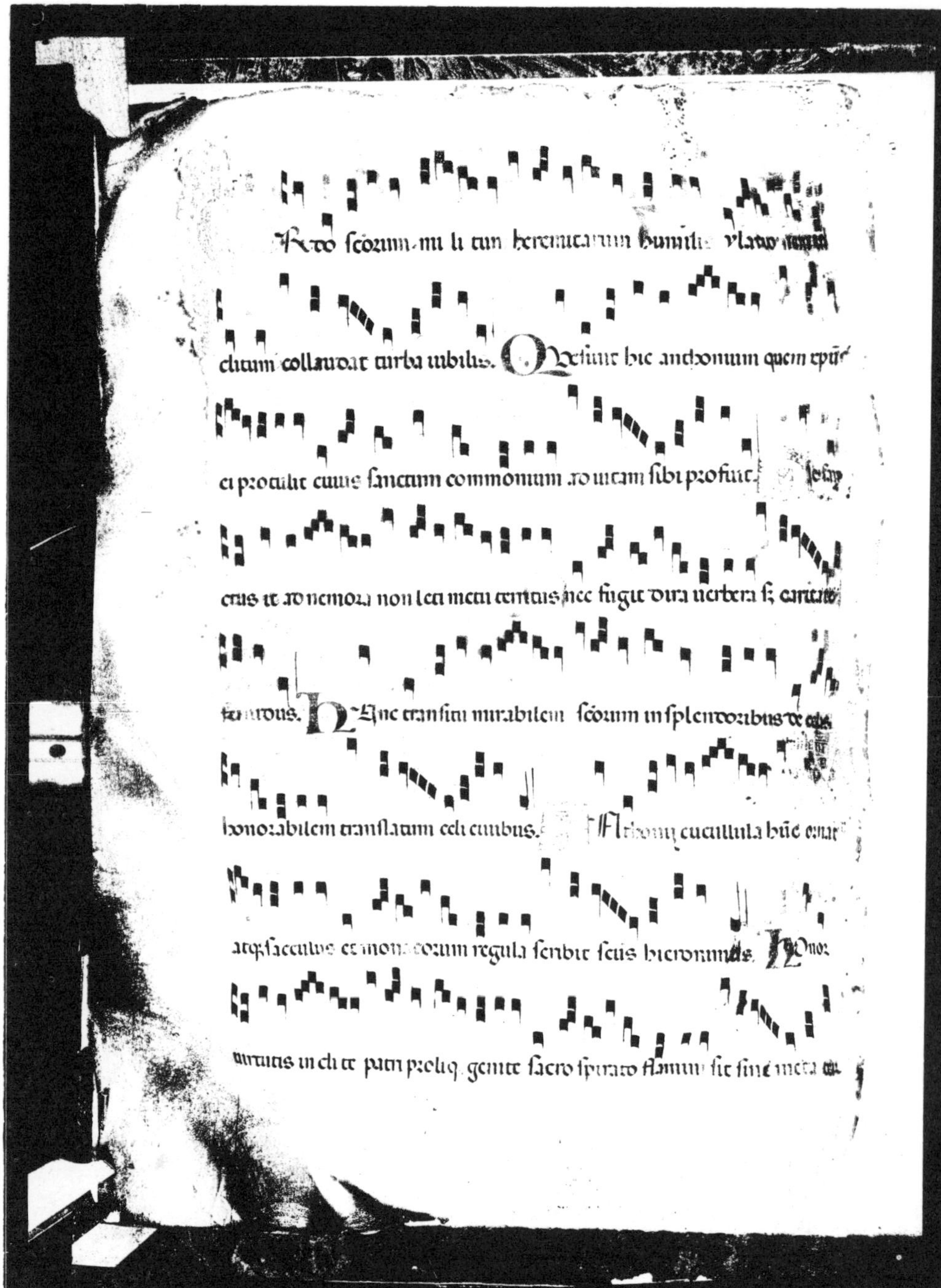

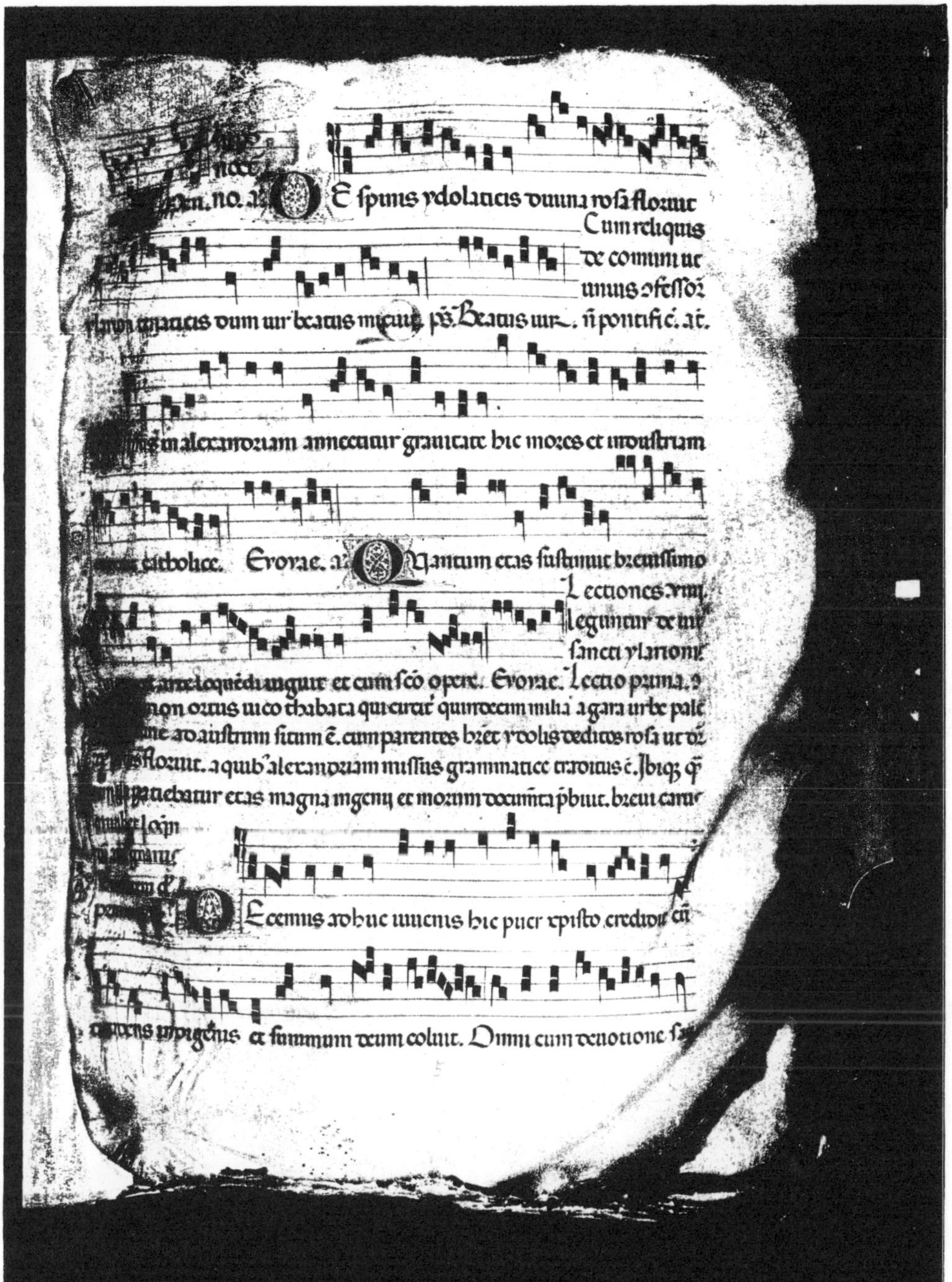

(Folio 4)

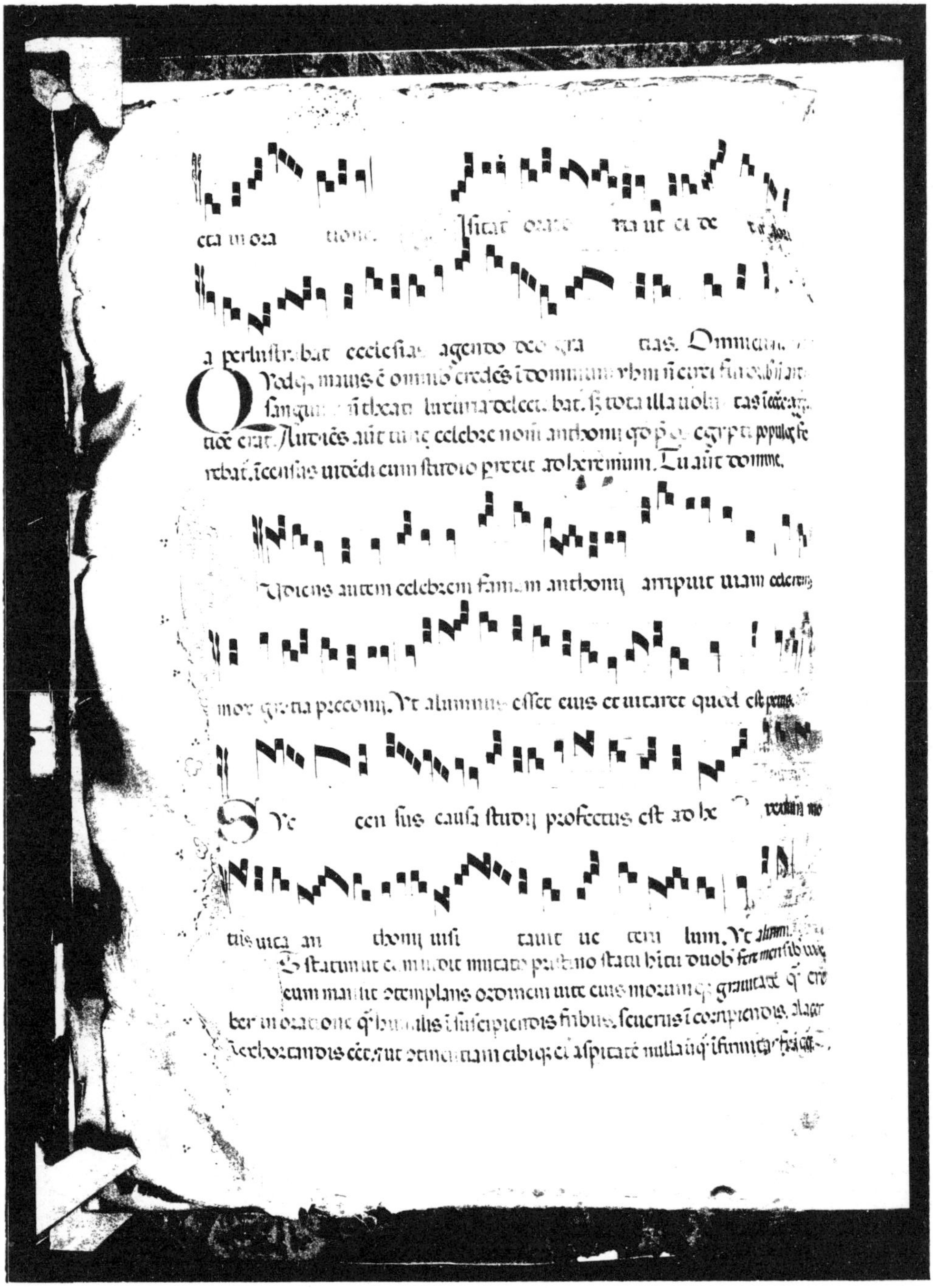

(Folio 5)

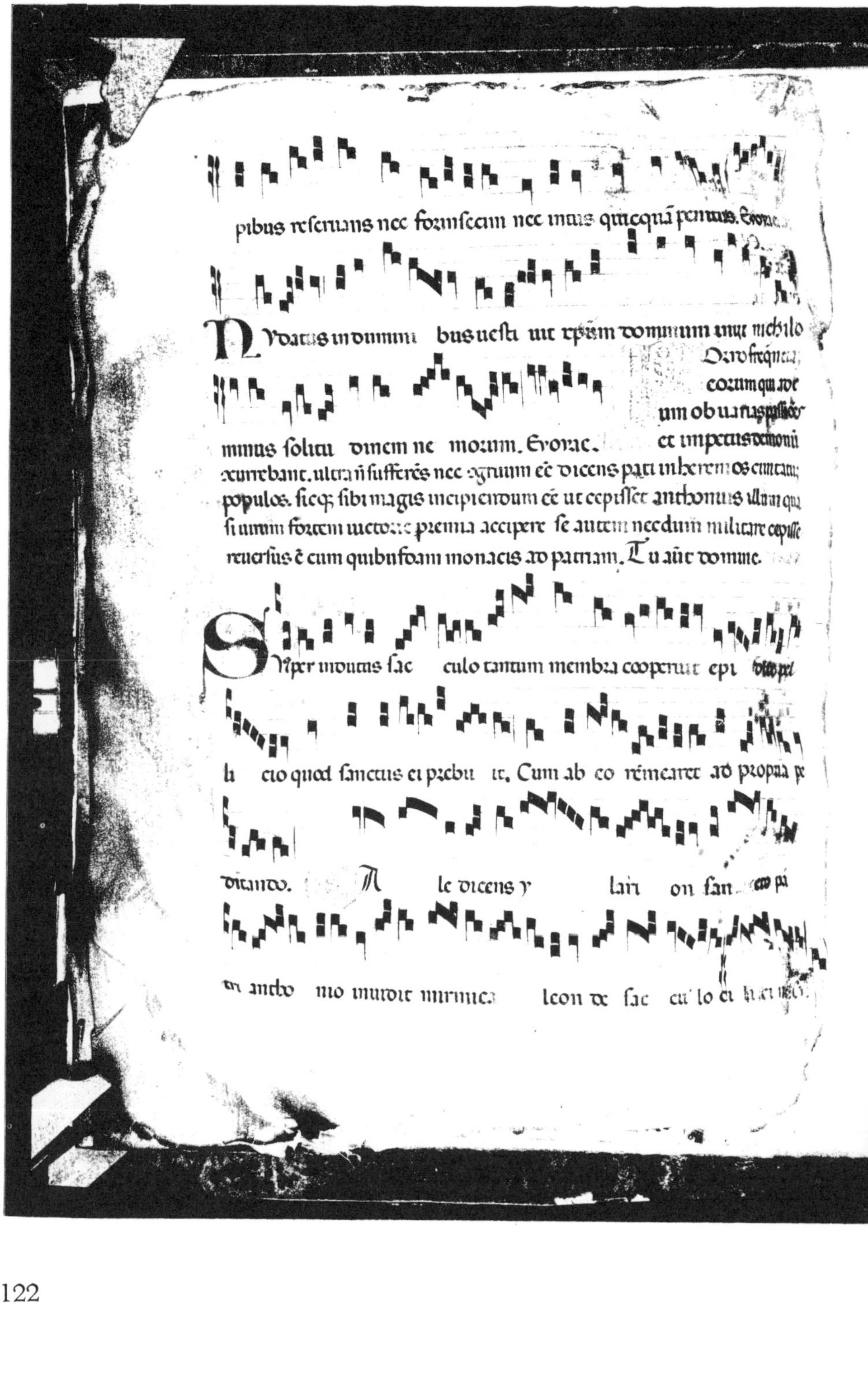

(Folio 6)

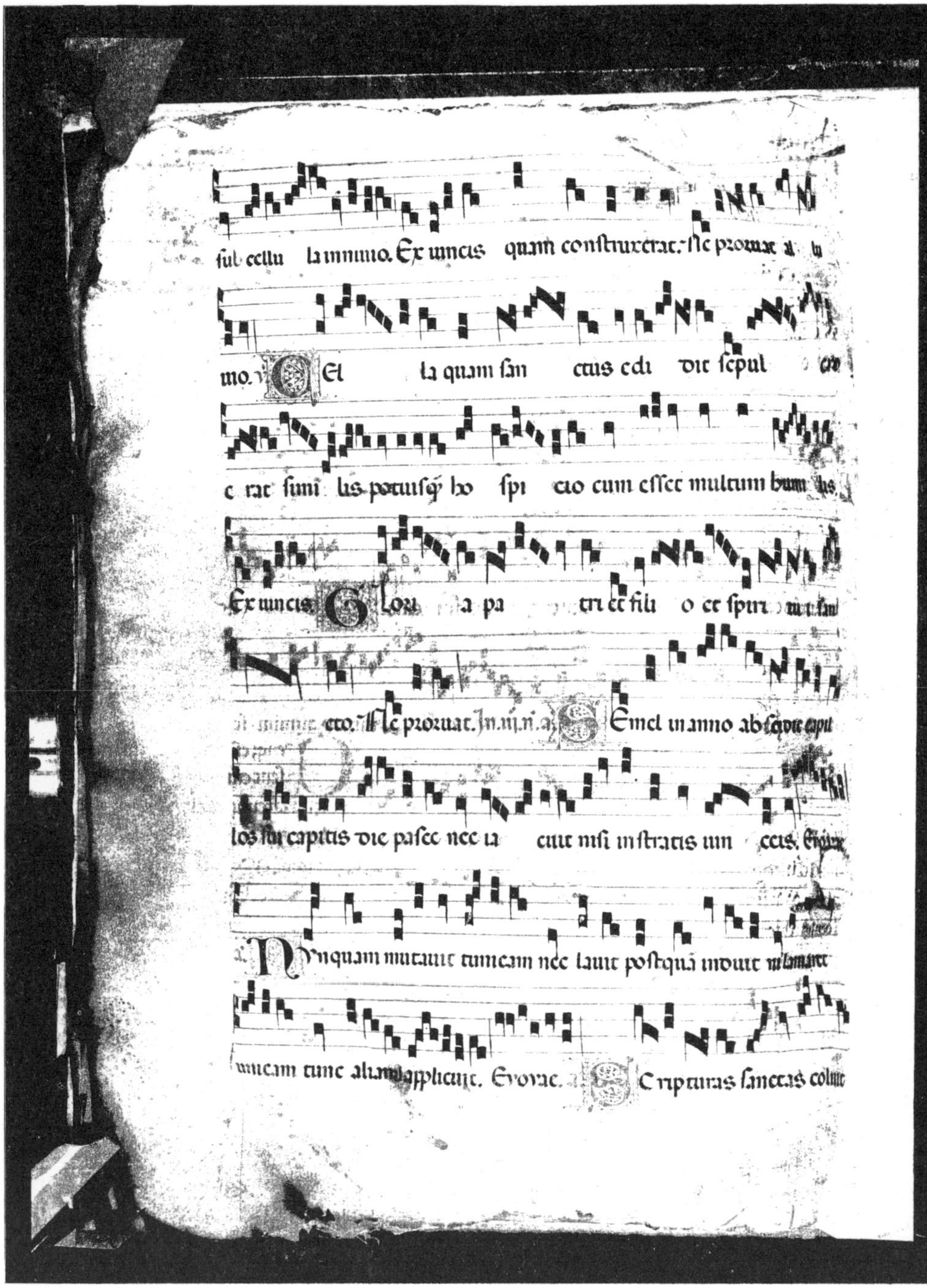
Ex iunctis quam construxerat.
la quam san ctus edi dit sepul
erat simi lis potuisse ho spi tio cum esset multum
Ex iunctis
Glori a pa tri et fili o et spiri
Semel in anno
los sui capitis die pasce nec la uit nisi in stratis iun ceis.
Nunquam mutavit tunicam nec lavit postquam induit
tunicam tunc
Evovae.
Scripturas sanctas colui

(Folio 7)

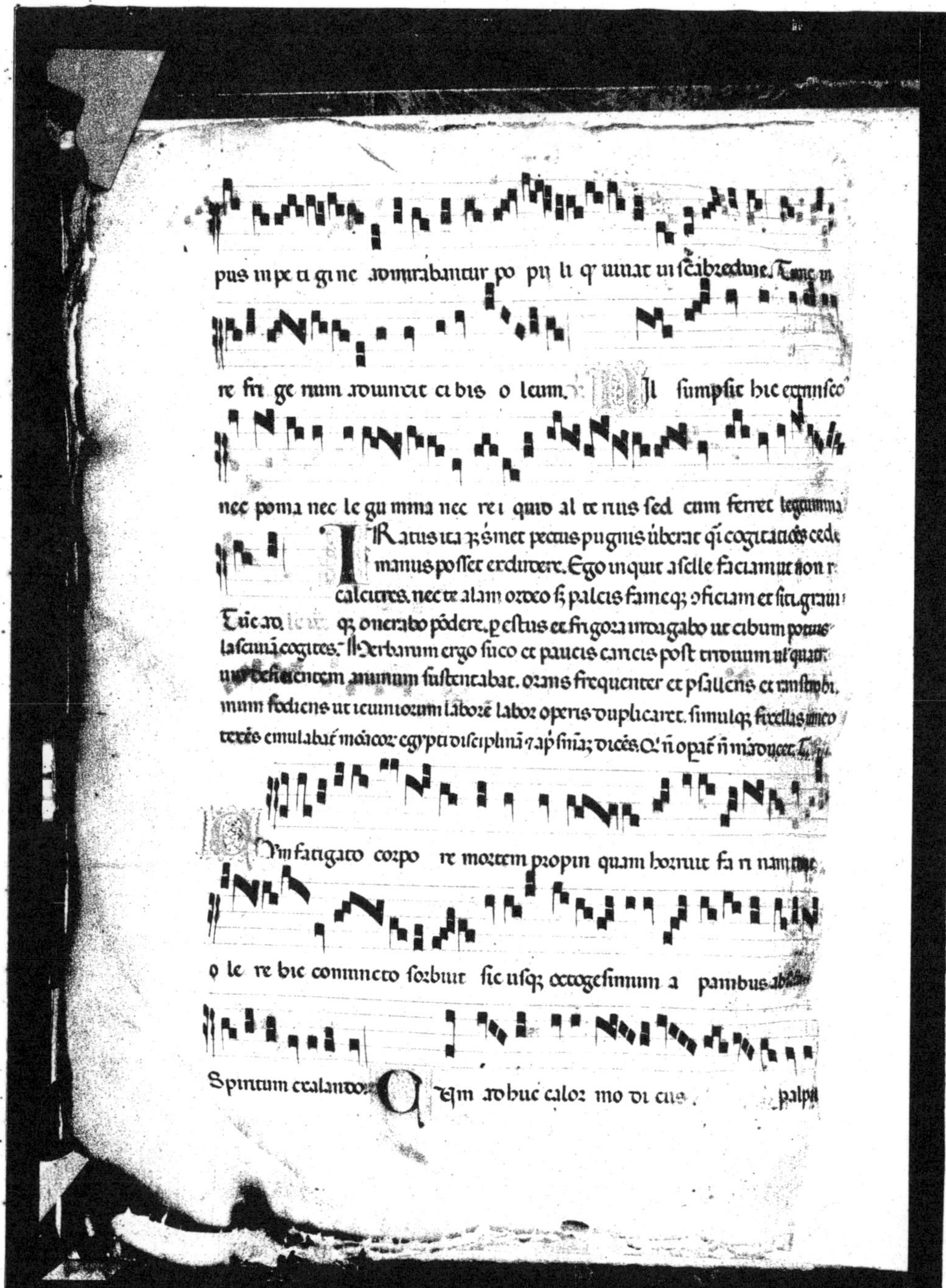

(Folio 8)

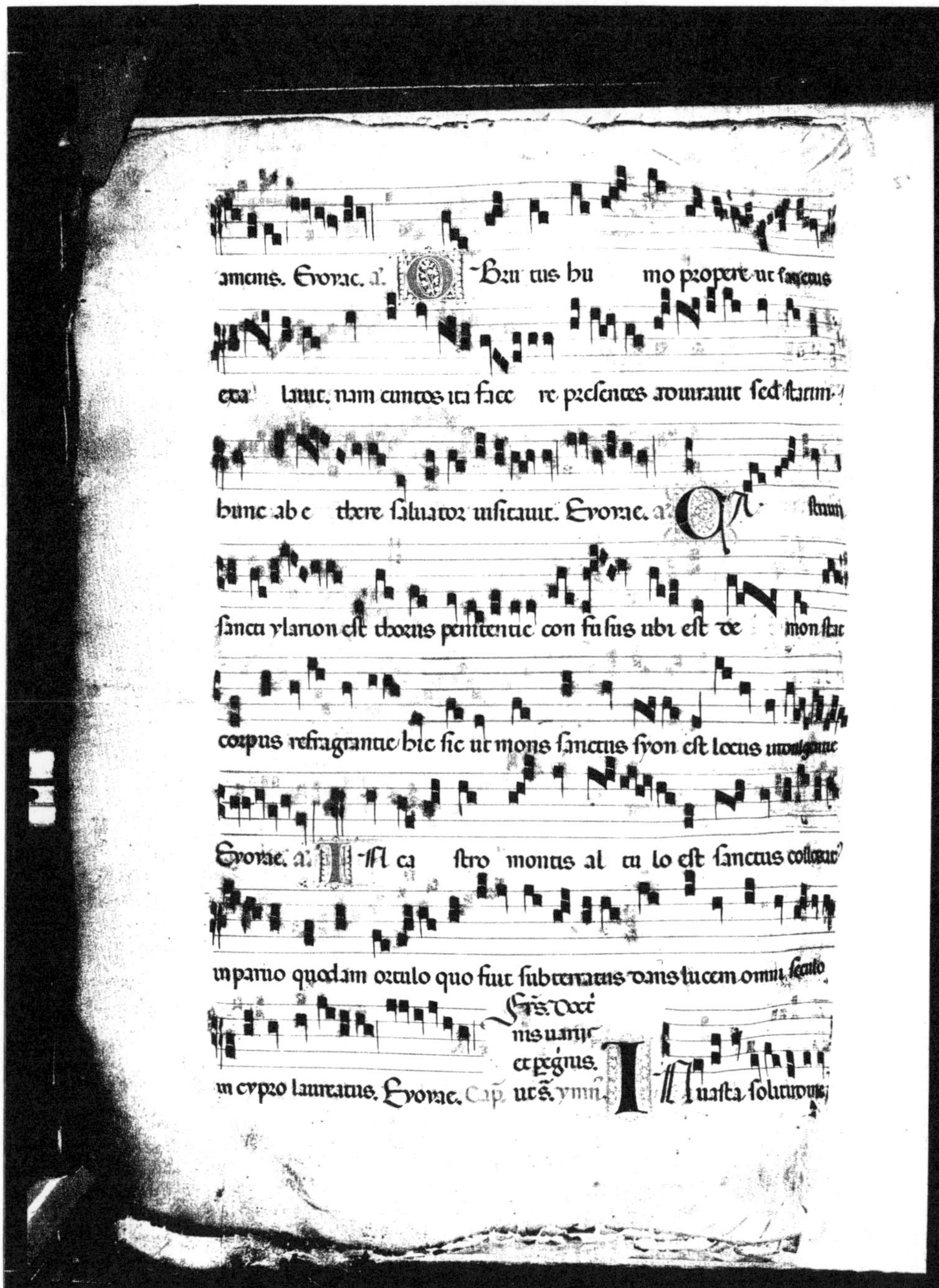

(Folio 9)

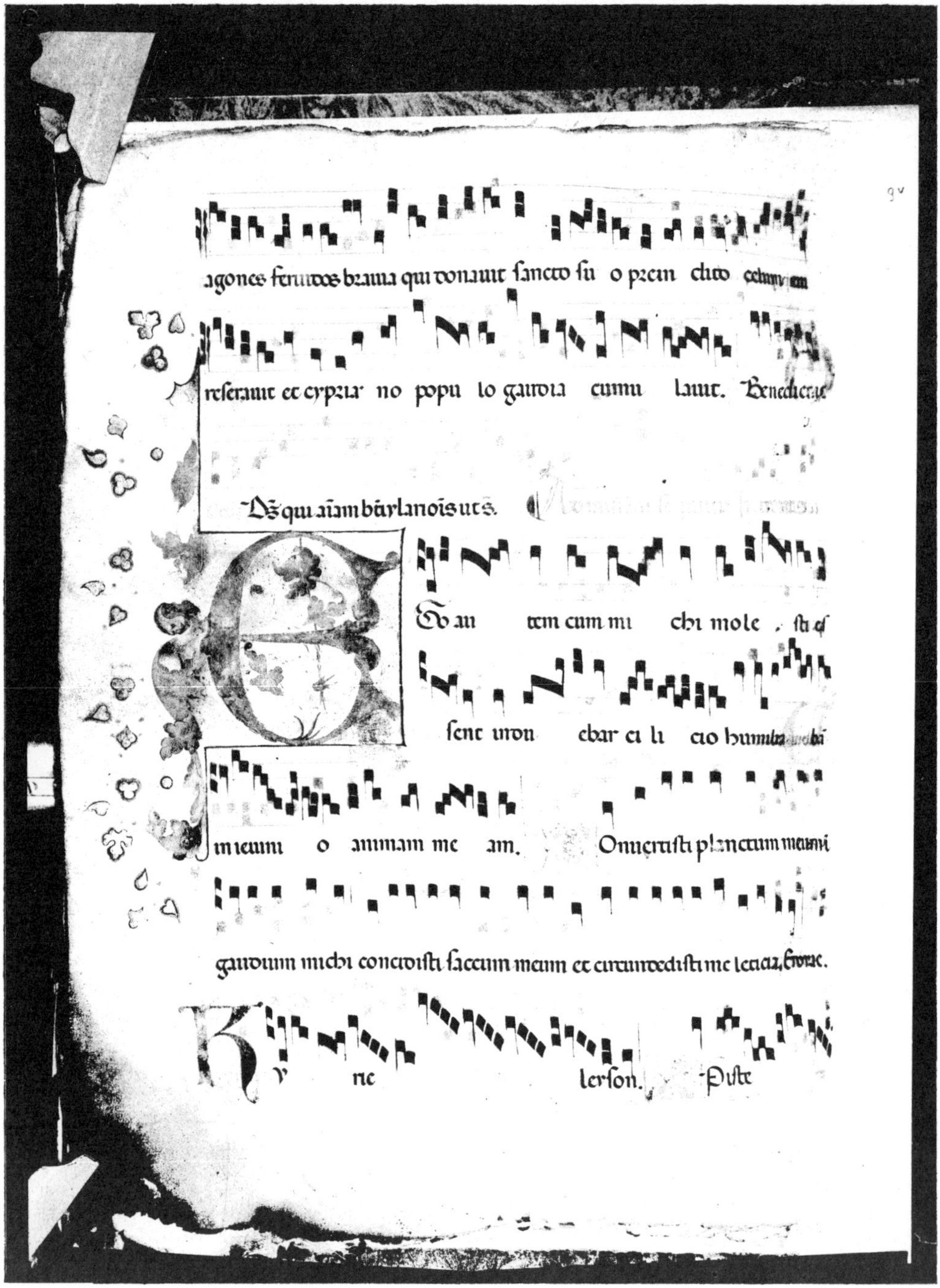

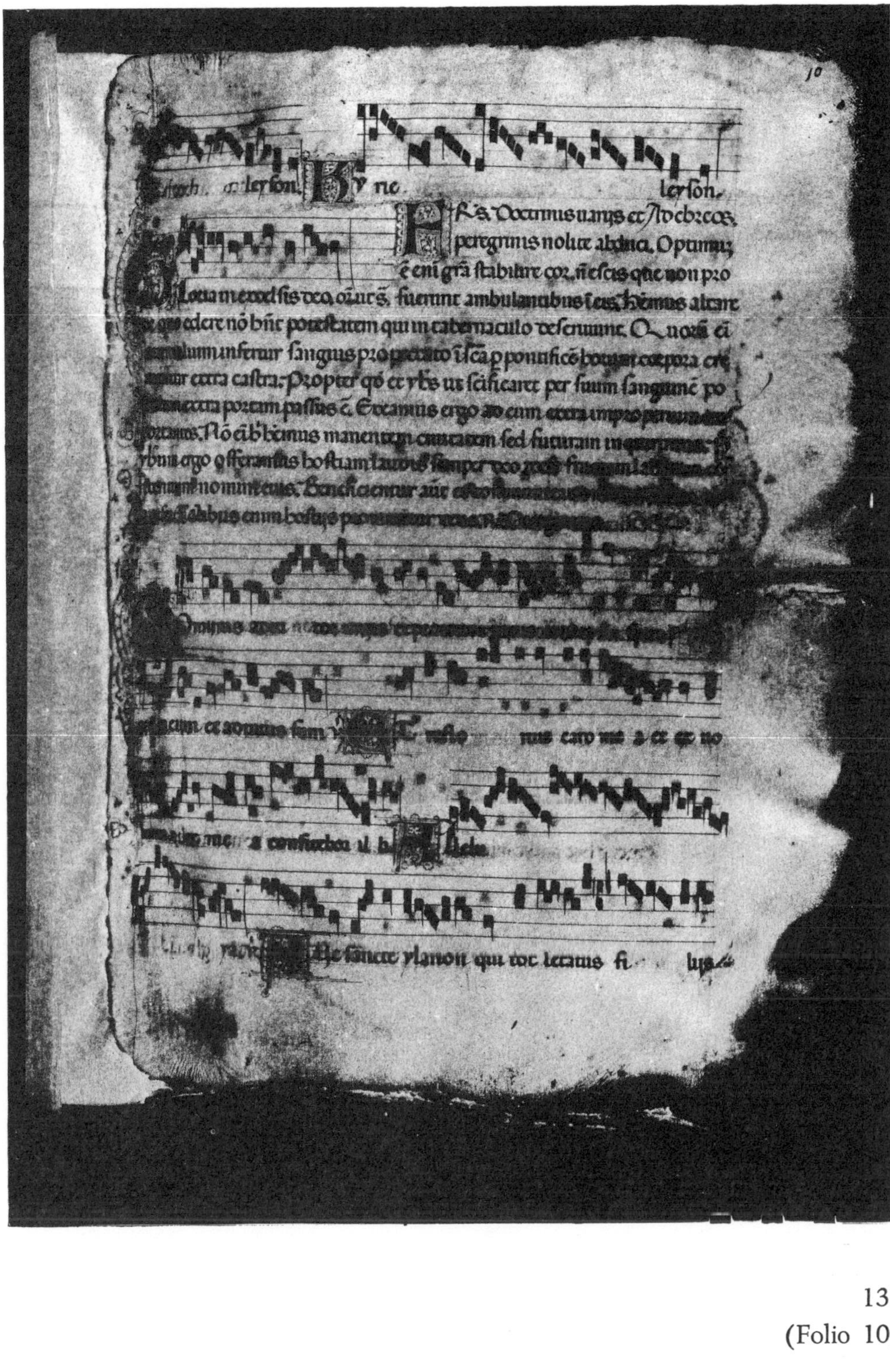

(Folio 10)

10v

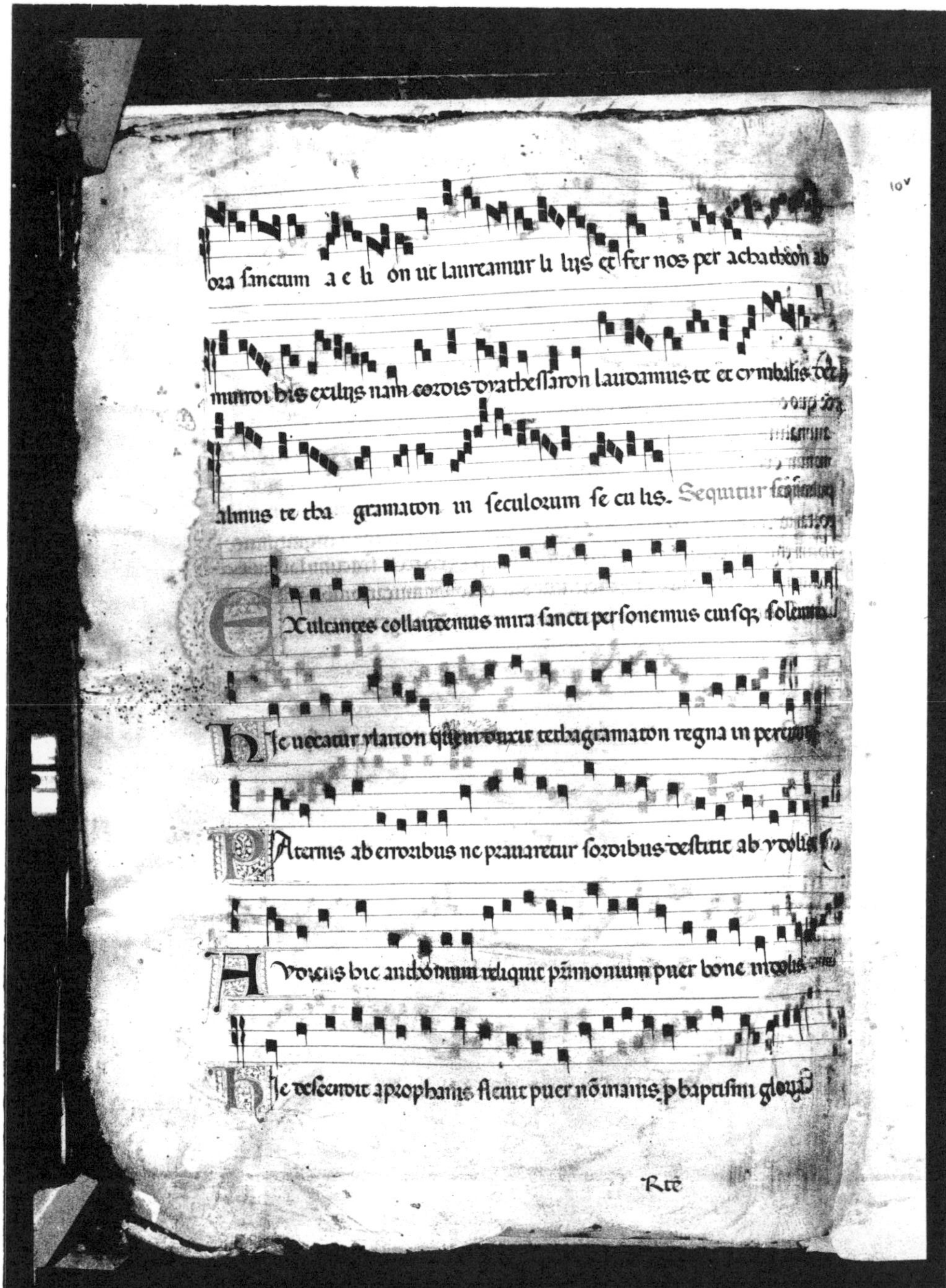

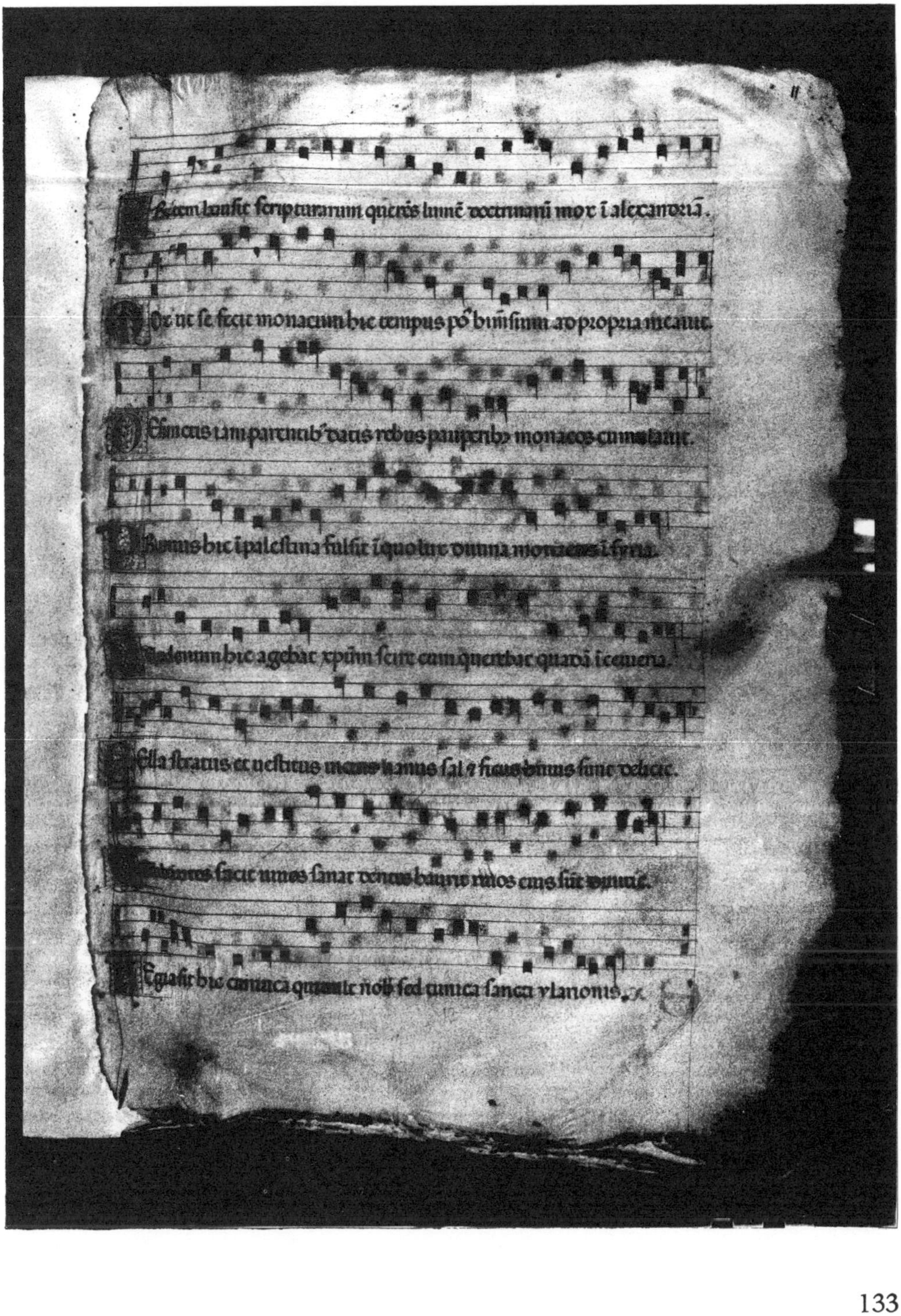

(Folio 11)

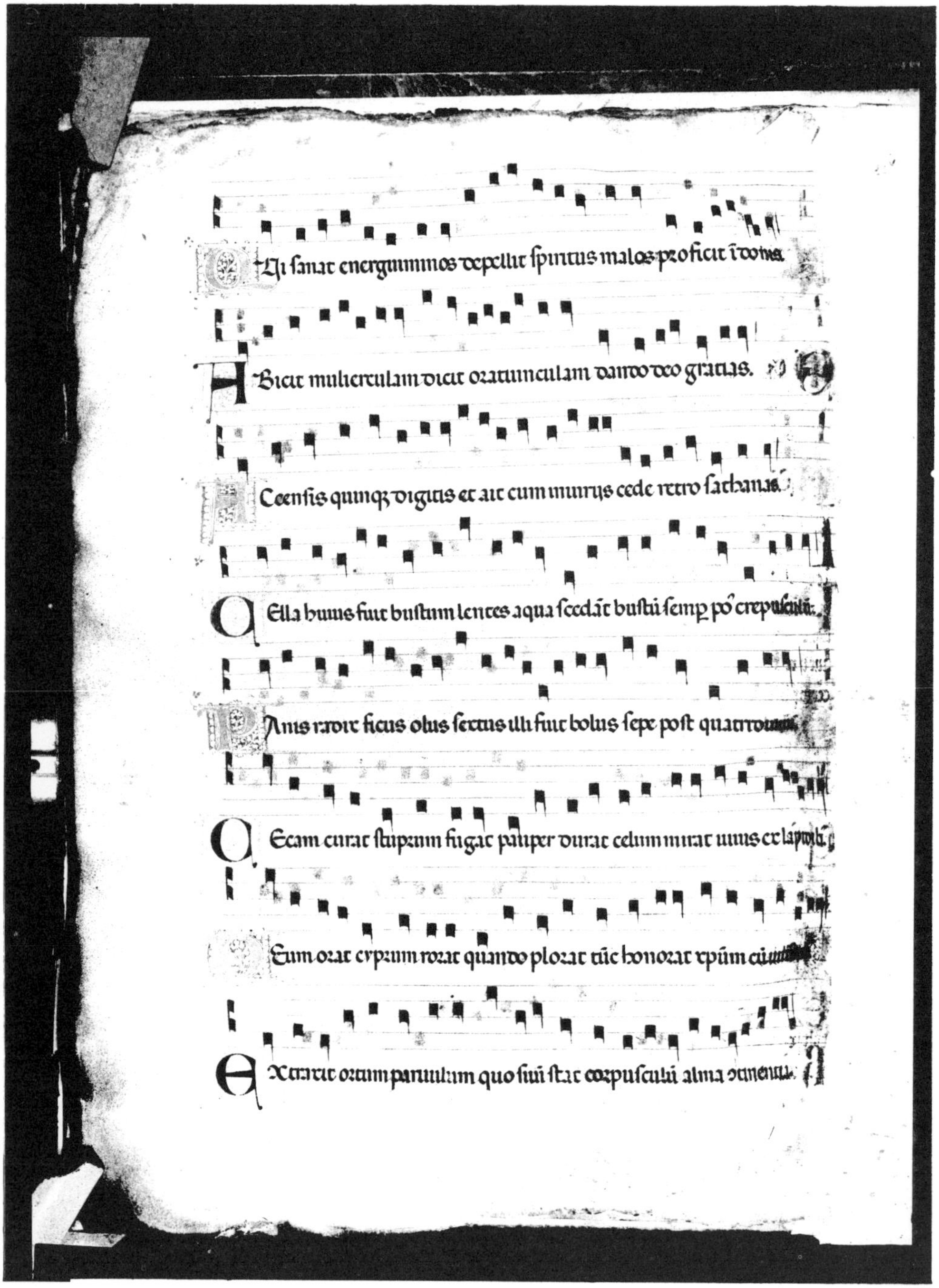

(Folio 12)

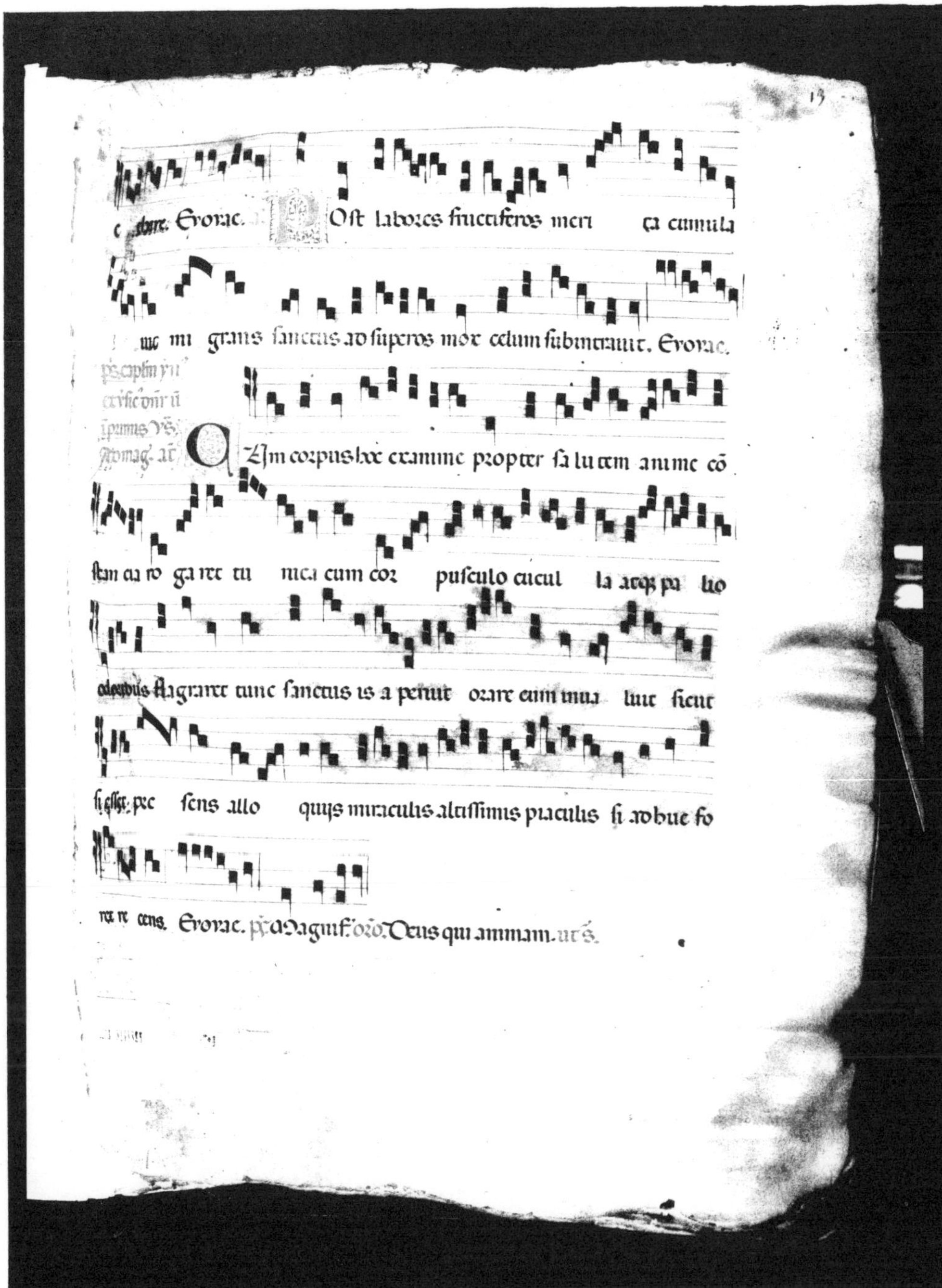

(Folio 13)

[BLANK]

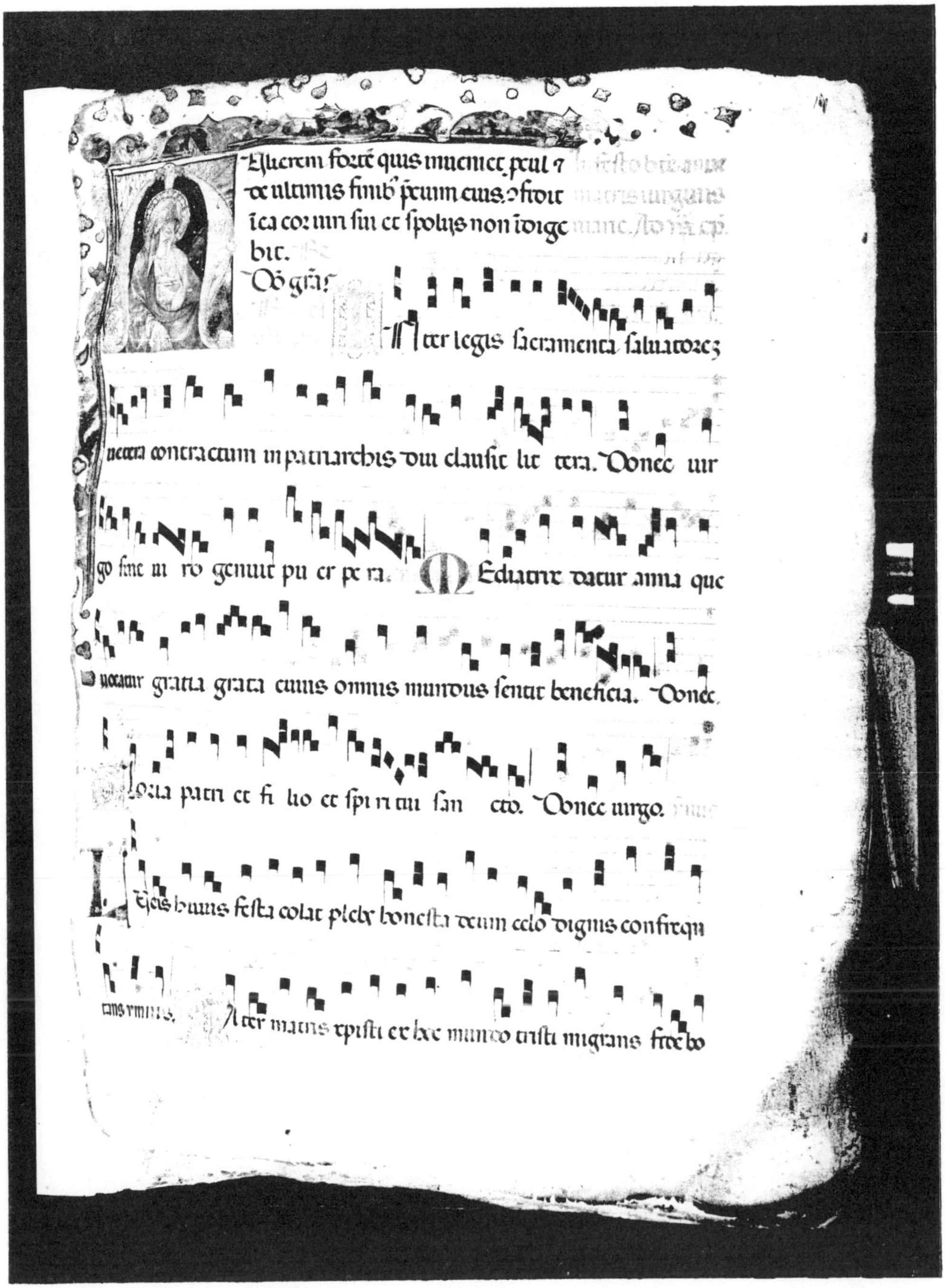

(Folio 14)

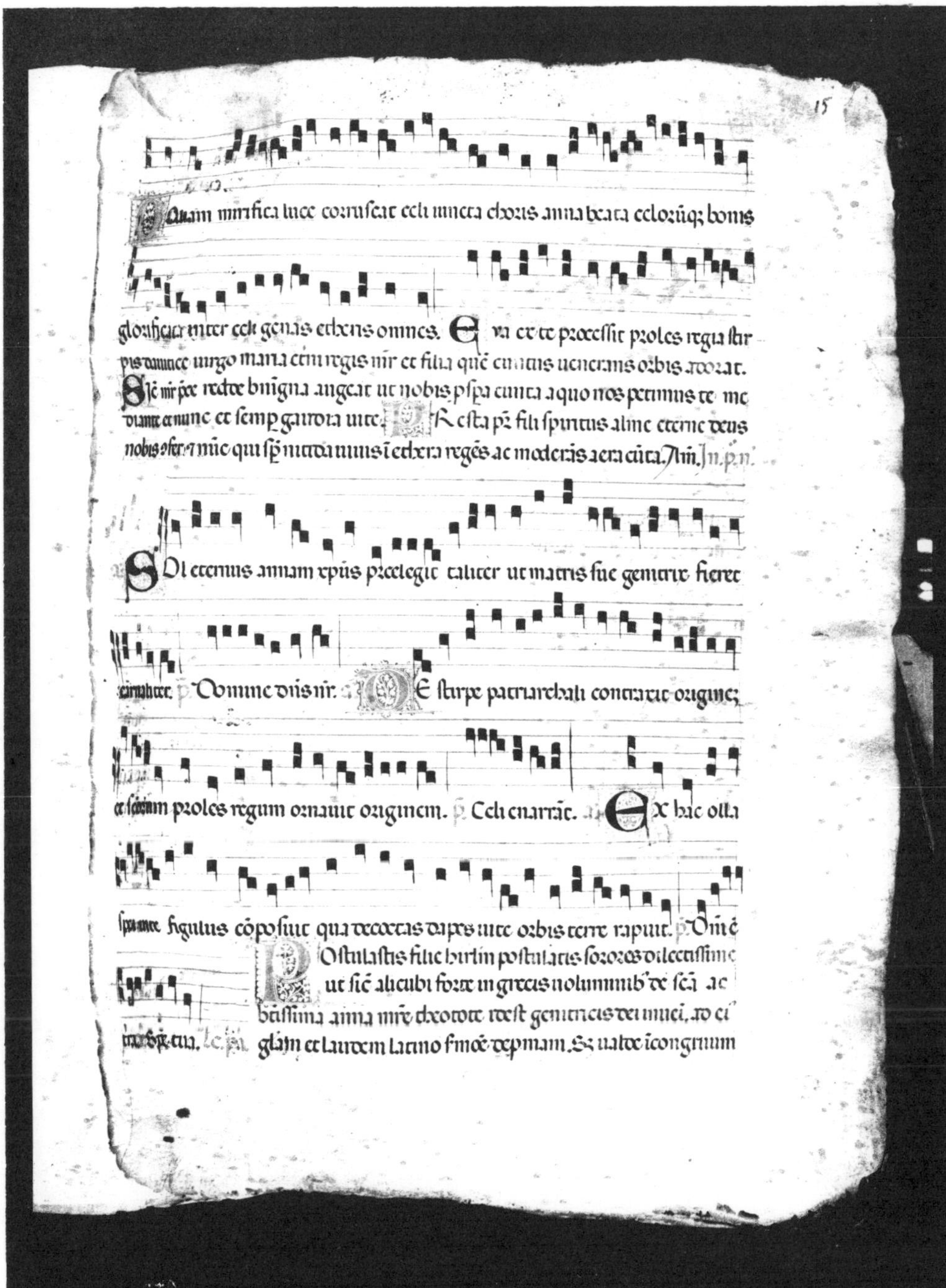

(Folio 15)

Anna felix uelut radix uiuit in arbore.
patiens amigdalum. Anna.
Bethleem natale solum
colitur. Que domus eterni panis et celestis dicitur.

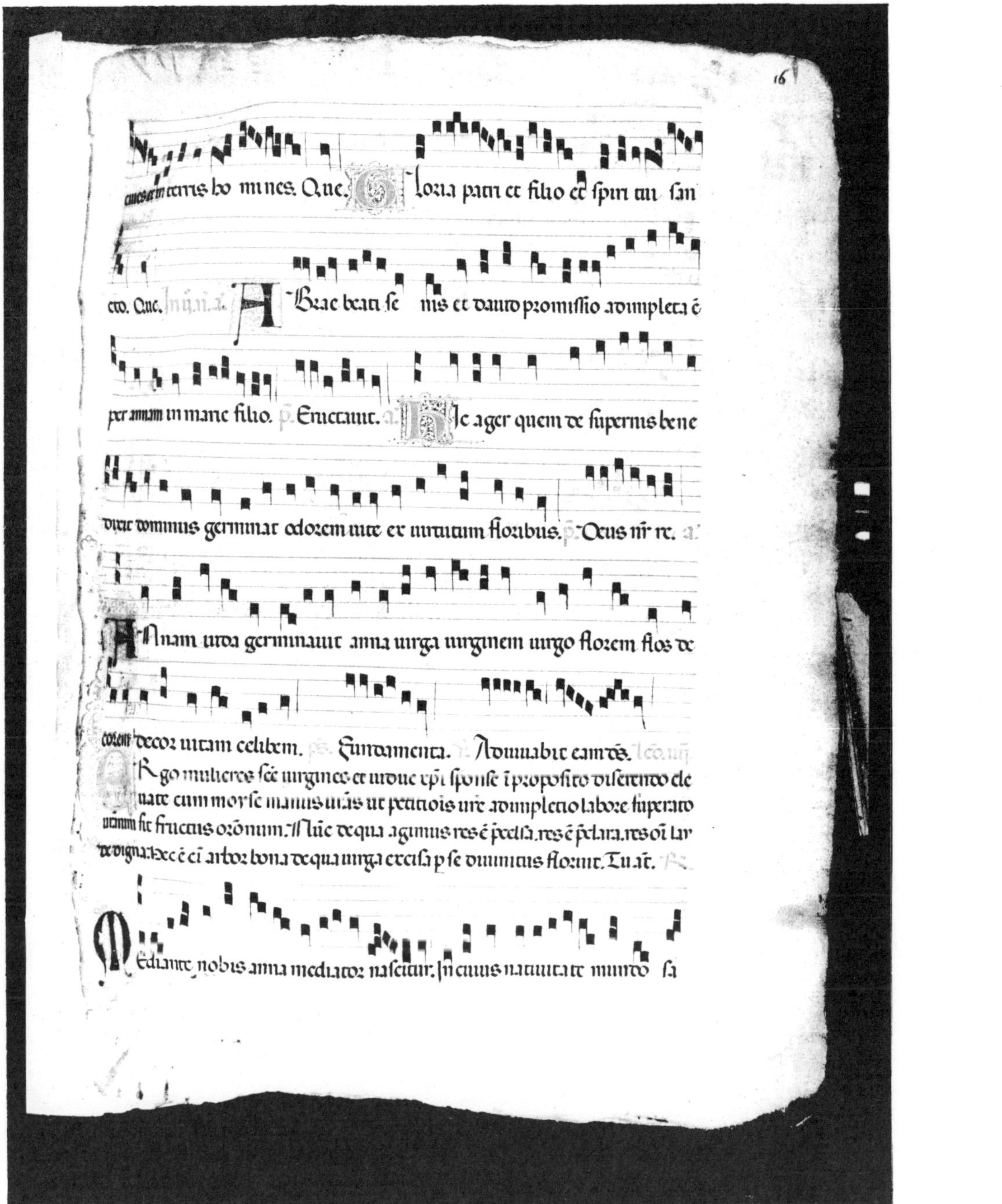

(Folio 16)

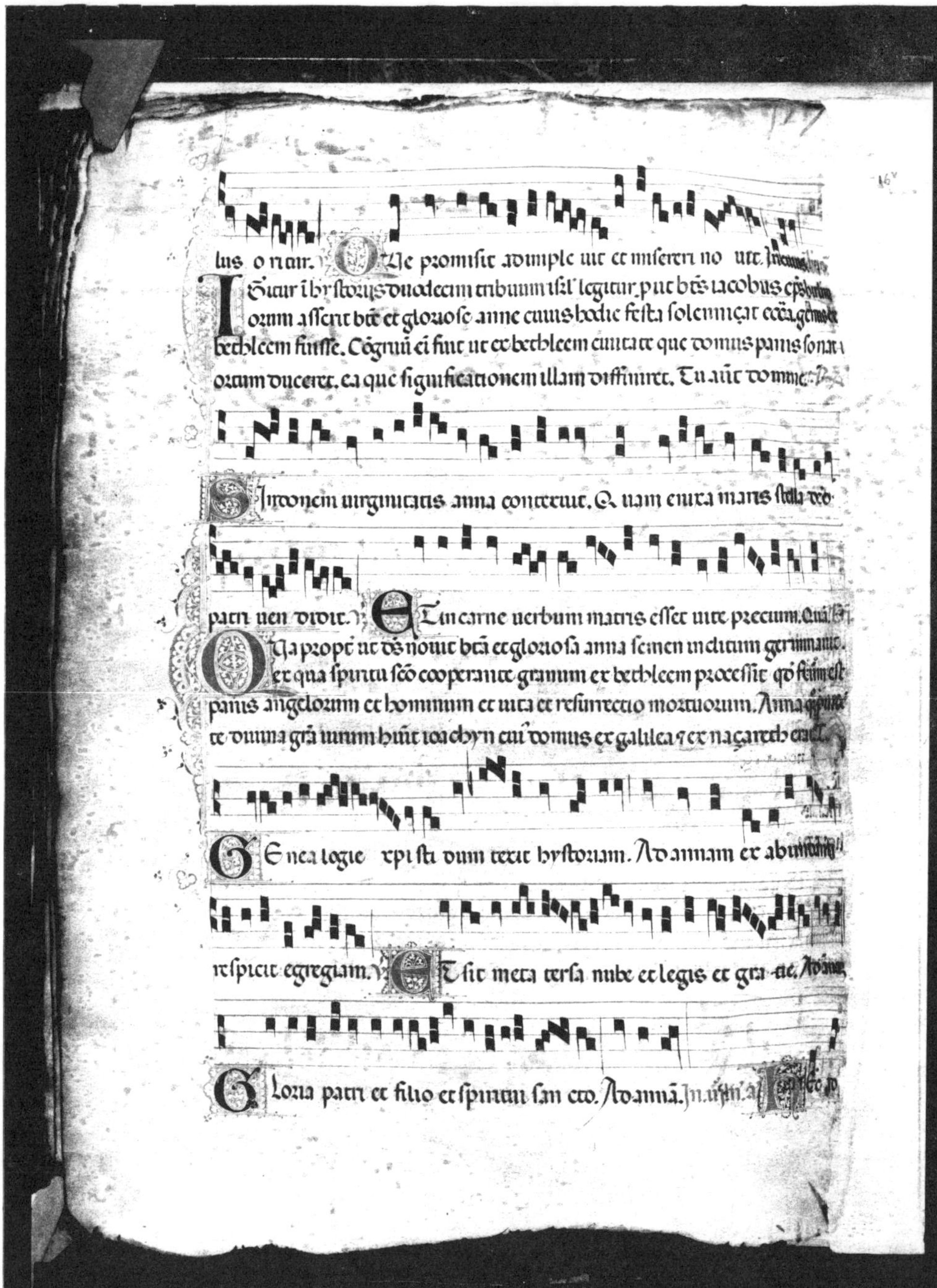

(Folio 17)

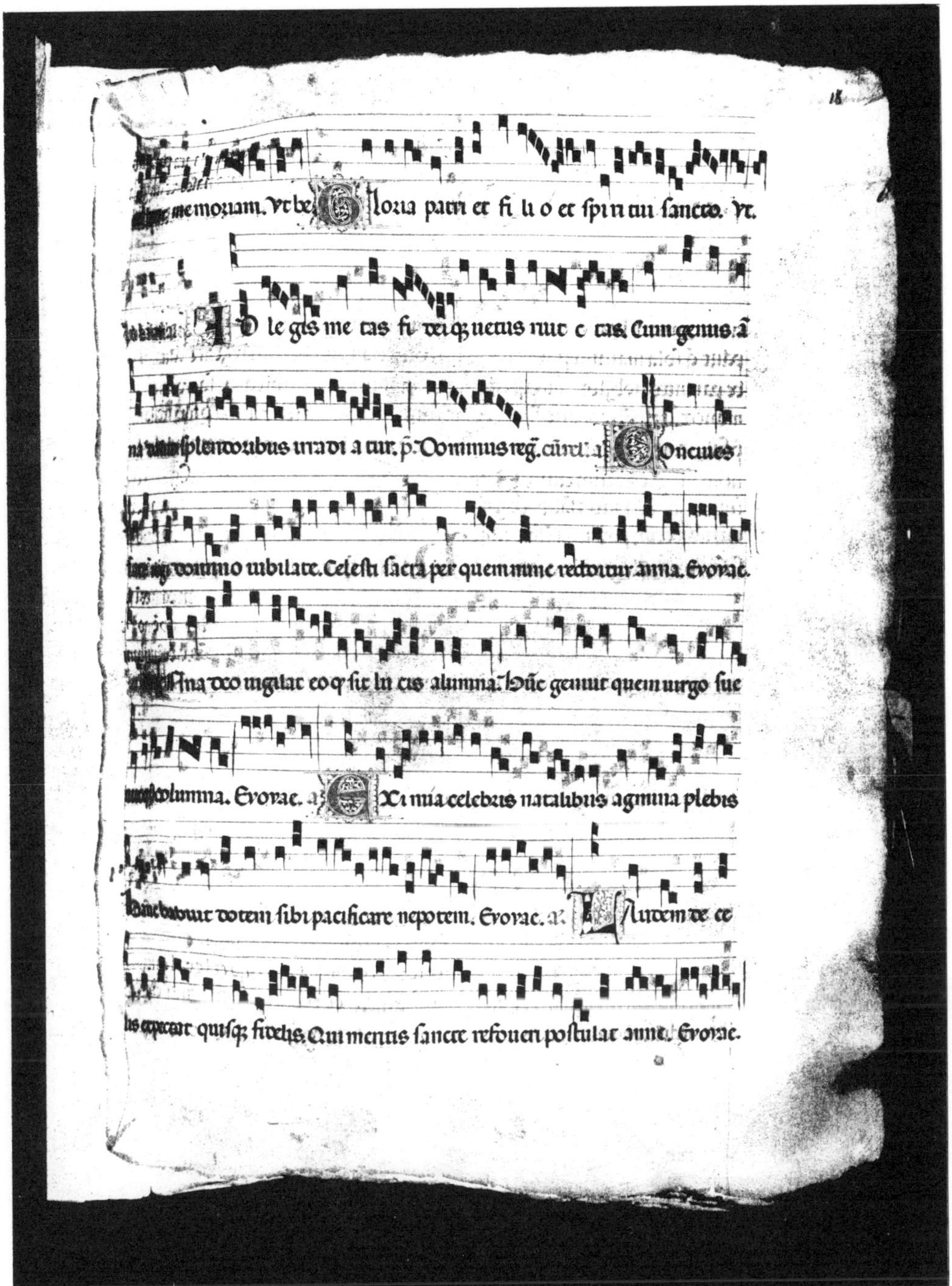

(Folio 18)

na pa rens ma tris de qua sapientia pa
tris incarnata dedit fidei quod mundus habebit. collige nos retis inter
sacra membra nepotis. Anna beatorum comes esto memor famulorum.

(Folio 19)

Kyri e leyson.
leyson. Kyri e
leyson.
Et in terra pax hominibus bone uoluntatis.
udamus te. Benedicimus te. Adoramus te.
orificamus te. Gratias agimus tibi propter
gnam gloriā tuam. Domine deus rex celestis deus pa
ter omnipōs. Domine fili unigenite yhesu xpe.

(Folio 20)

xpistum filium dei unigenitum
omnia secula.
de deo uero.
per quem omnia facta sunt.
nram salutem descendit de celis.
tu sancto ex maria uirgine et homo factus est.
tiam pro nobis sub pontio pilato passus et sepultus
resurrexit tercia die secundum scripturas.

(Folio 21)

21v
Sanctus. Sanctus. Sanctus
sabaoth. Pleni sunt celi et terra gloria tua o sanna
Benedictus qui venit in nomine domini o sanna
qui tollis peccata mundi
Kyrie
leyson. Xpiste
leyson. Kyrie
leyson.

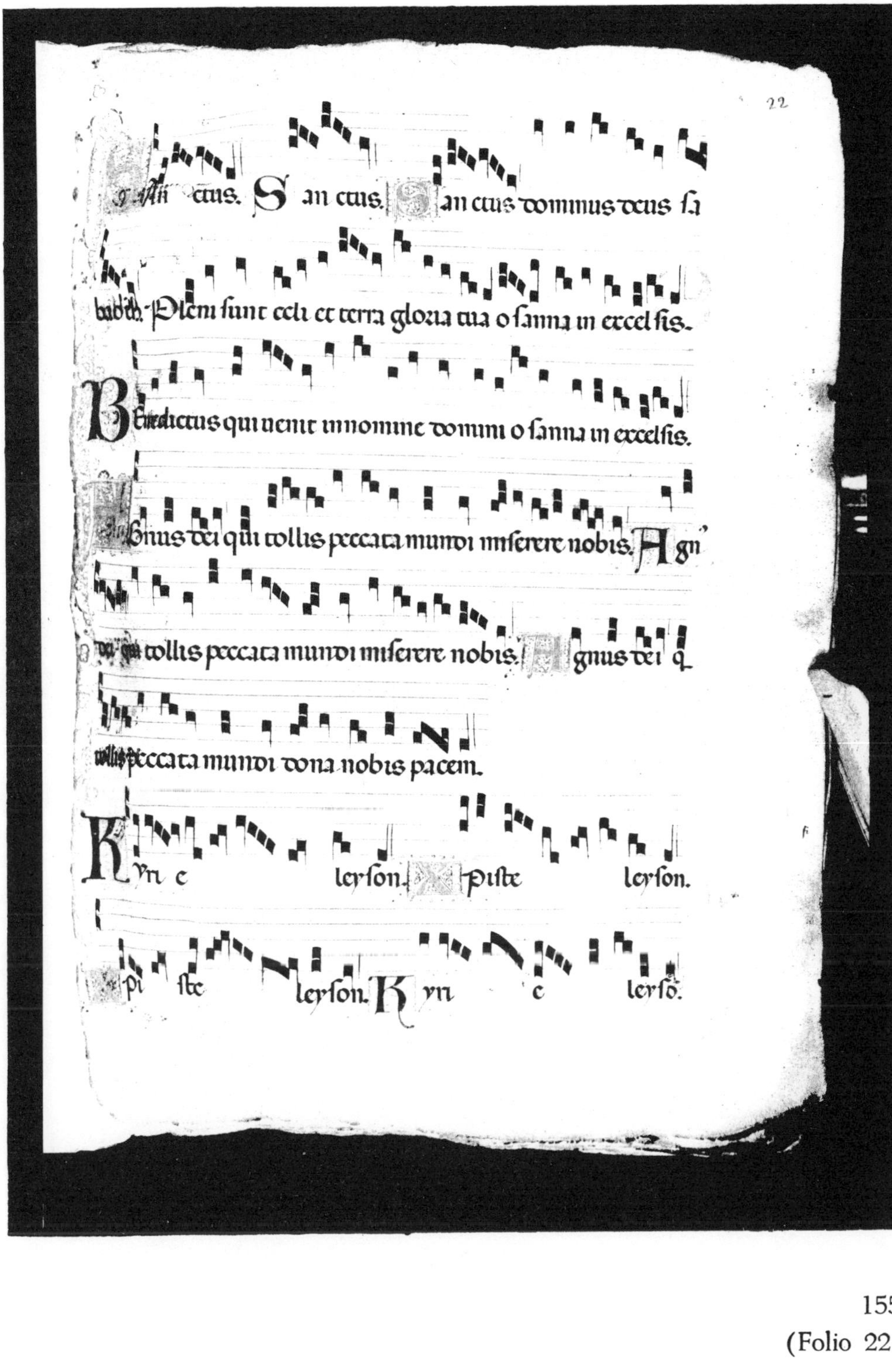
Sanctus. Sanctus. Sanctus dominus deus sabaoth. Pleni sunt celi et terra gloria tua osanna in excelsis.
Benedictus qui venit in nomine domini osanna in excelsis.
Agnus dei qui tollis peccata mundi miserere nobis. Agnus dei qui tollis peccata mundi miserere nobis. Agnus dei qui tollis peccata mundi dona nobis pacem.
Kyrie eleyson. Christe eleyson.
Christe eleyson. Kyrie eleyson.

(Folio 22)

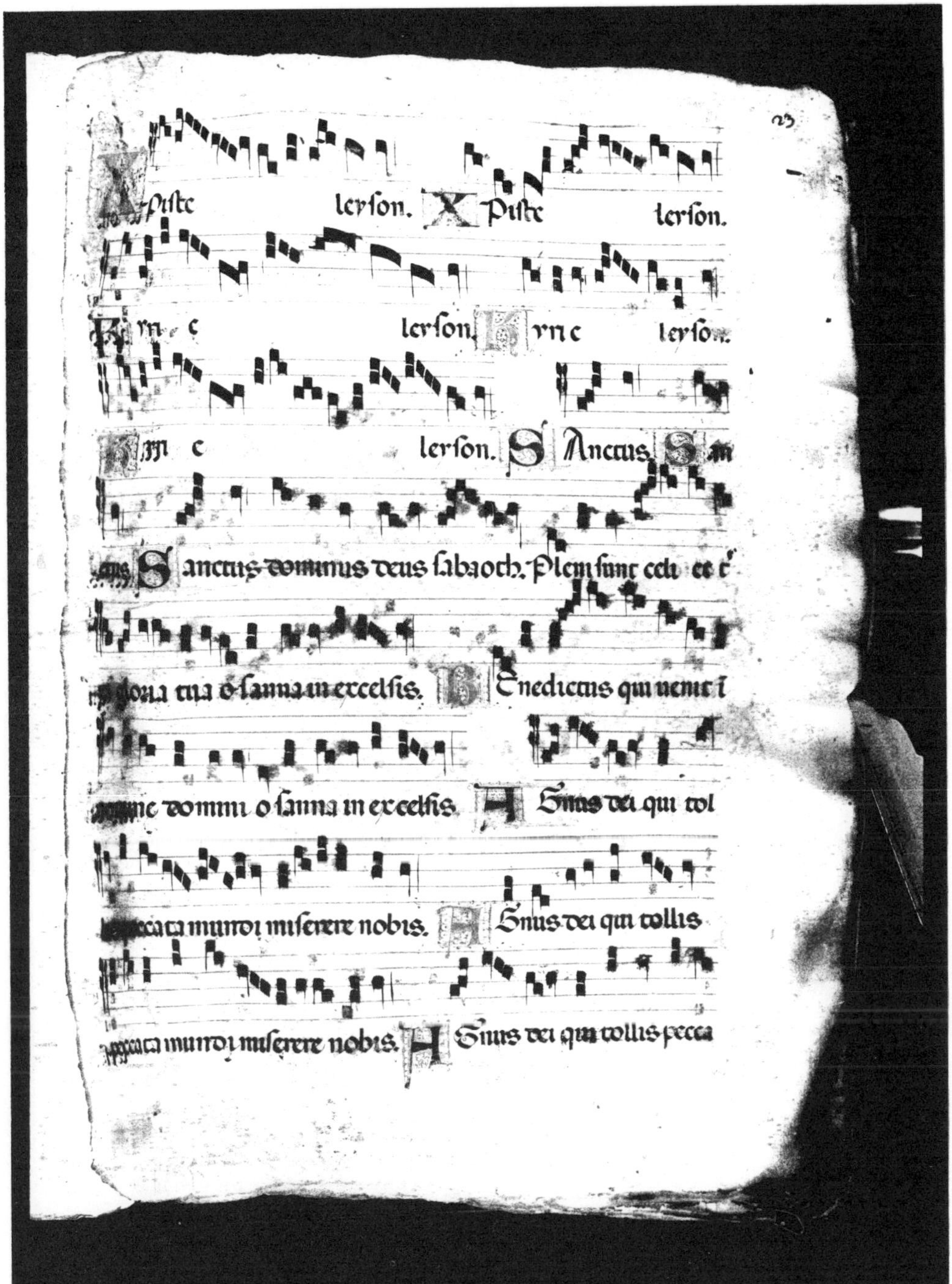
Xpiste leyson. Xpiste leyson.
leyson. Kyrie leyson.
leyson. Sanctus.
Sanctus dominus deus sabaoth. Pleni sunt celi et
gloria tua osanna in excelsis. Benedictus qui uenit
nomine domini osanna in excelsis. Agnus dei qui tol
peccata mundi miserere nobis. Agnus dei qui tollis
peccata mundi miserere nobis. Agnus dei qui tollis pecca

ta mundi dona nobis pacem.
Kyrie leyson. Kyri e
leyson. Xpiste leyson. Xpiste
leyson. Kyri e leyson. Kyri e
leyson. Kyri e leyson.
Et in terra pax hominibus bone voluntatis.
mus te. Benedicimus te. Adoramus te. Glorifica
te. Gratias agimus tibi propt' magnam glori
ā tuam.

rex celestis deus pater omnips. Domine fili uni
genite yhesu xpiste. Domine deus agnus dei filius pris.
tollis peccata mundi miserere nobis. Qui tollis peccata mūdi
deprecationem nrām. Qui sedes ad dexteram patris
nobis. Quoniam tu solus scūs. Tu solus domin
solus altissimus yhu xpe. Cum sancto spiritu i glori
patris. men.
atrem omnipotentē factorem celi et terre uisibilium omniū

(Folio 24)

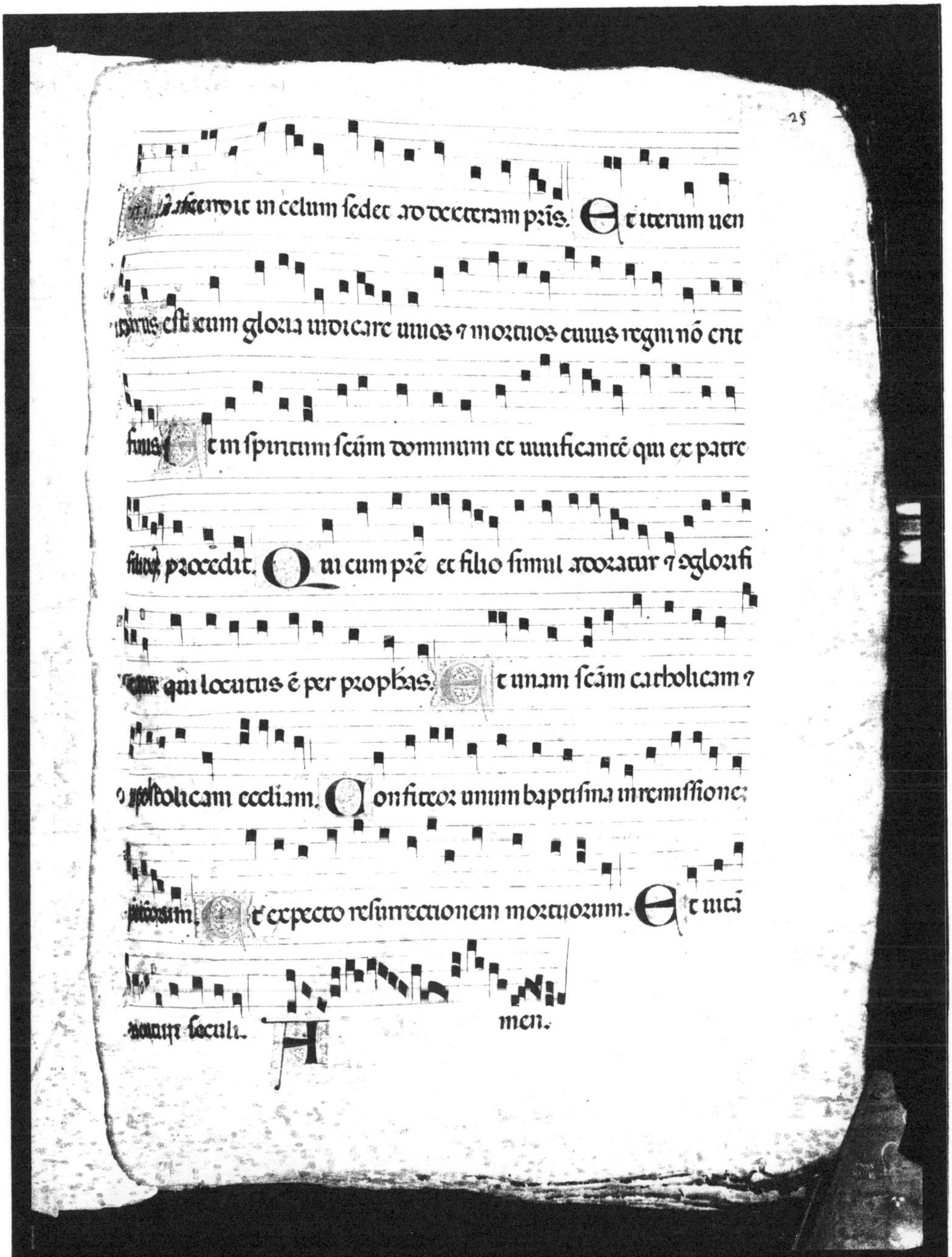
25
in celum sedet ad dexteram pris. Et iterum uen
est cum gloria iudicare uiuos et mortuos cuius regni nō erit
Et in spiritum scm̄ dominum et uiuificantē qui ex patre
procedit. Qui cum pr̄e et filio simul adoratur et glorifi
qui locutus ē per prophas. Et unam scām catholicam et
ecclīam. Confiteor unum baptisma in remissionē
Et expecto resurrectionem mortuorum. Et uitā
seculi. A men.

San ctus. San ctus. San ctus dominus de
us sabaoth. Pleni sunt ce li et terra gloria tu a osanna in ex cel
sis. Benedictus qui venit in nomine domini osanna in excel
sis. Agnus de i qui tollis peccata mundi miserere nobis
Agnus dei qui tollis peccata mundi miserere nobis.
de i qui tollis peccata mundi dona nobis pa cem.
Kyrie leyson. Kyrie leyson.
leyson. Xpiste leyson.

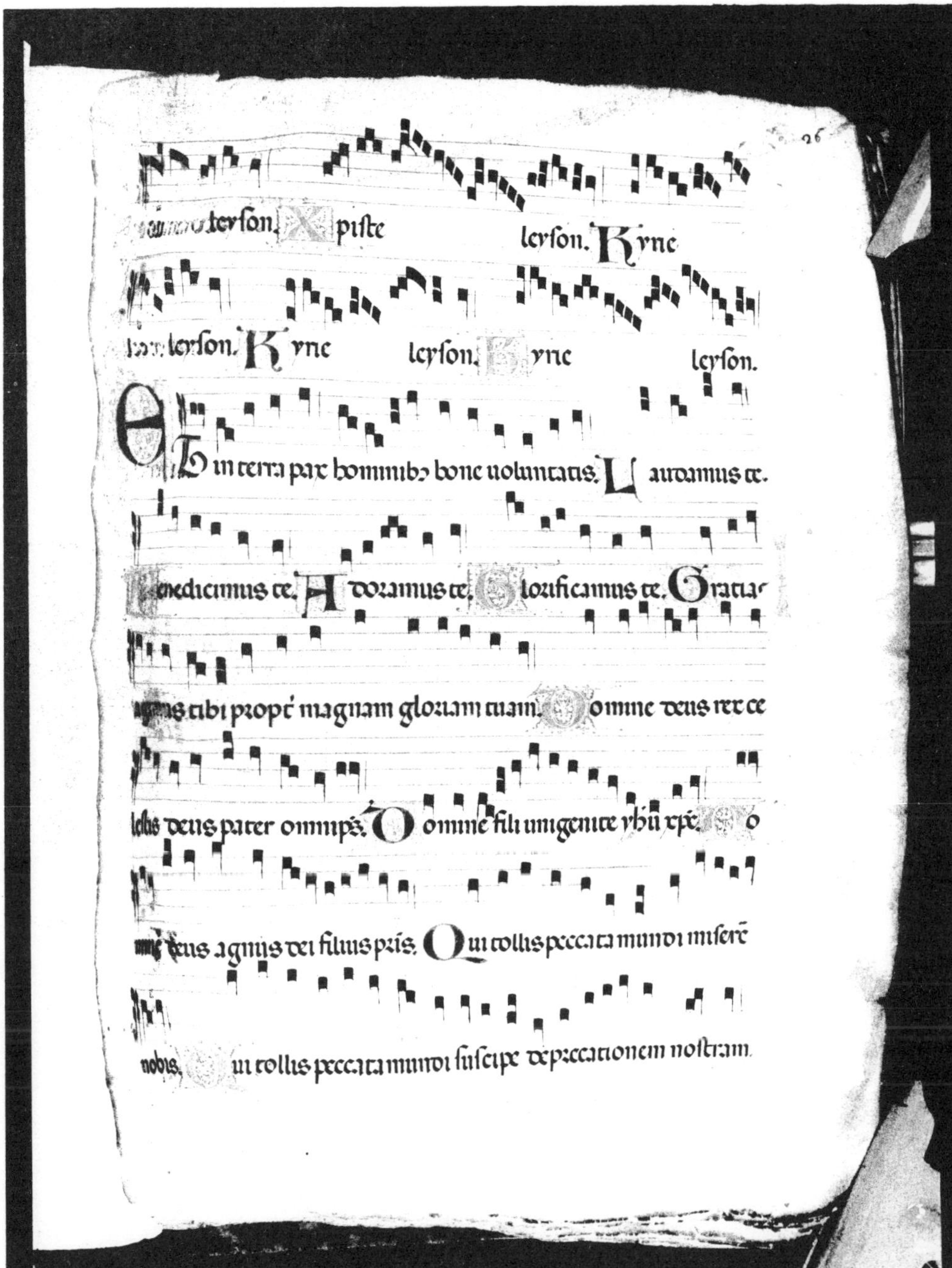

(Folio 26)

(Folio 27)

(Folio 28)